THE INTEGRITY CODE

THE INTEGRITY CODE

A Spiritual Blueprint
For Creating
Meaningful Success

Francis de Geus

LTP
PUBLISHING

Contents

Introduction

One morning I woke up, and there it was. No dream, just these three words: *blueprint for success*. I wrote them down and knew this was the title of a book, and I knew I had to write it. But since I had little experience as a writer, it took some time to work up the courage to decide to take this on.

First, I became curious. Then my curiosity became like an itch that won't go away until you scratch it. I really wanted to know: *Is there a blueprint for success?*

To discover the answer, I went on a fact-finding mission. I read books about success, I asked God to show me, and I interviewed people. The interviews resulted in my own very unscientific experiment: I asked people to rate themselves on a scale of 1 to 10 where 1 means they hate their life, and 10 that they love it.

Then I asked them why. Little by little certain principles began to stand out. As I rearranged them into some kind of order, a pattern emerged.

This book is my honest effort to show you this pattern.

Stories are the heart of this book. Stories about rich and famous people and stories about regular people like you and me. Hidden inside these stories are clues. Timeless principles that create a pattern that governs our lives.

There is no shortage of books about success, yet this book is different. It takes a look at the spiritual component that plays into success. How important is spirituality as we strive for success? And how can we live in this world and be successful in a spiritual way?

It's the spiritual component that addresses the meaningful side of success.

What's meaningful is different for different people, but that doesn't mean there is no rhyme or reason to it. What is meaningful changes over time, not at random, but in a certain direction. In a more spiritual direction.

That's at the heart of the book. How we change, over time, for the better. And how both we and others benefit from this change. How much we change varies from person to person, because this change does take effort. Some people are willing to put in a lot of effort, others only a little, and some none at all.

Our lives will reflect the work we put into this process.

According to a 2023 survey by the Pew Research Center, 70% of U.S. adults think of themselves as spiritual. Many of them have had a spiritual experience. Spirituality has historically been linked to various religions, but our society is changing and becoming more secular. As churches stand empty, a sizable and growing segment of society are people who have no connection with organized religion, yet they do feel a spiritual connection.

What, then, does it mean to be spiritual?

It's something that defies hard definitions. In my mind spirituality is something we discover. It happens when we become aware of being connected to something greater than ourselves. An awareness that this universe is more than a lot of atoms floating aimlessly through space.

Some people list experiences such as feeling a connection with people who have died. Sometimes they even receive a communication from their deceased loved ones. Some have had a near death experience, or other out-of-body travel that gave them a deeper understanding of the spiritual nature of this universe and our role in it. Some experience a deep spiritual connection through a sense of divine love. And in some cases, people experience an inner light or sound that uplifts them. It's different for different people, but it always connects us to a higher and larger purpose. It is what makes life meaningful.

Victor Frankl became famous for writing *Man's Search For Meaning*. In it he writes about his experiences as a Jew in several German concentration camps. He believed that our primary motivation in life is the search for meaning. After the war he helped many individuals find purpose and meaning in life's often hard experiences. By doing so, he was able to help lift them out of a state of depression. Being able to perceive meaning in our experiences is important to our well-being. It's not always easy to do.

I wrote this book from the perspective that life *is* meaningful. And if this is true then there is a difference between meaningful success and its counterpart, meaningless success. Meaningless success leaves you empty and unsatisfied, like eating a meal that doesn't seem to fill you up. Meaningful success fills you with satisfaction. It makes you feel good. Meaningful success is what we are looking for, but sometimes we lack the discernment to know the difference.

I don't claim to be an expert on success. I have no titles to show my expertise. And though I can't claim to have the final word on success, I do have one thing. I love my life. It's not as impressive as a title, but I wouldn't trade it for any title in the world, no matter what perks come with it.

I believe that *meaningful* success leads to that—loving your life.

Finding success is a journey, and to make that journey there are three essential components.

To use an analogy, let's compare this journey to a road trip. What do you need? Besides a car, you need fuel, a roadmap and a destination.

Part one of the book delves into the head and the heart. The heart is essential, because it contains your why. This is your fuel on the road to success.

Part two is a roadmap of sorts. Here we look at the natural progression of life. We evolve and grow, not at random, but in a predictable way. There are stages we go through as we develop into a more mature, functional adult. It's a journey of refinement, where we learn to value what is meaningful.

Part three is the destination. It's where the natural progression of life takes us: integrity. It's a spiritual blueprint. An ideal that is worth the effort, because it is the key to meaningful and lasting success.

The better we are at incorporating this ideal into our life, the more successful we can be in manifesting the life we want.

We all have a shot at this, and it is my hope that this book will give you the tools and insights to make it your best shot.

Part One

The Head and the Heart

We don't have one major center of intelligence and decision making, but two: the head and the heart.

Chapter 1

What is Meaningful Success?

You know you are on the road to success if you would do your job and not be paid for it.

—Oprah Winfrey

Warren has a particular way of making sure he loses weight when his pants are getting too tight. He gives his kids an unsigned $10,000 check with the promise that if the weight doesn't come off in the next month, he will sign their checks.

Not once did his kids get to cash their checks. Not losing the weight would violate his two rules of business: Rule #1: Never lose money. Rule #2: Never forget rule #1.

To say that Warren is obsessed with money is putting it mildly.

As a ten-year-old, he boldly proclaimed he would be a millionaire by the time he was thirty-five. A book he found in the local library, *One Thousand Ways to Make $1,000,* set him on his way. It planted in his mind the concept that became the hallmark of his success: compound interest. It is the idea that profits, when reinvested, will lead to exponential returns over time.

It was all he needed to get started.

He began making money as a six-year-old selling chewing gum door-to-door. From there he progressed to peanuts and popcorn during football games and selling secondhand golf balls. He collected wastepaper and magazines from the neighborhood to sell for scrap. He shoveled snow, worked in his granddad's grocery store, and helped to unload a truck with fifty-pound bags of animal-feed. After unloading the truck, he walked away saying that manual labor is for the birds.

What suited him much better was delivering papers. He delivered the *Washington Post* and the *Times-Herald* in the morning and later added the *Evening Star* in the afternoon. He was always reading and thinking, and delivering the papers gave him time to think.

He made his first investment in the stock market when he was barely twelve years old and ended up making a small profit.

Warren spent none of the money he made. He had a different goal in mind. He wanted to be independent and work for himself. He didn't like the idea of other people telling him what to do. Money to him meant freedom. And it was important to him to have the freedom to do what he wanted every day.

Warren Buffett made good on his prediction as a ten-year-old and made his first million by the time he was thirty. And he was only getting started.

Time and business-savvy would eventually make him the richest man in the world. Worth an estimated $62 billion in 2008, he gave away billions to charitable organizations, which set him back to a still respectable #2 spot on the *Forbes* list.

Warren's story is unusual. Few people have made it to the *Forbes* list, and fewer still to the top of the list.

It begs the question: Is money the ultimate scorecard for success?

Walter Williams' answer is a resounding "no."

Walter stands about six feet tall, wears stylish glasses, and is usually dressed better than the other people in the room. His curly hair is greying, giving him a distinguished look.

When I asked Walter to score his life on a scale of one to ten, with one meaning *I hate my life* and ten *I love my life*, he immediately said ten. Then he paused for a moment and went for a nine instead, realizing there is always something that can improve. But clearly this guy is extremely happy with his life.

What immediately stands out about Walter's story is that at two weeks old, he was adopted. His adoptive parents loved him, gave him a good home, and he was always grateful for that. As a child he was aware of his adoptive status, but rather than feeling less than his peers because of it, he felt special because he had been chosen. His parents certainly gave him the right message.

Even now that he's a parent himself it is still what he's most grateful for in his life.

"It inspired me to want to work with children as a psychologist. I majored in psychology with the intention of getting my master's and PhD, and to be working with children in a clinical setting."

He worked as an intake specialist in a children's home with the intention of continuing his studies. But when his career took a surprise shift towards fundraising for the children's home, he decided to stick with that and let go of his aspirations for continuing his college education.

It hasn't stopped him from feeling connected with the children and the mission of the children's home.

"I'm very proud of what I do and of the organization that I work for. It's nice to be a force for good, a person that represents moral values, that generally the world is moving away from. And to help children shape their futures to be successful and to have love and happiness in their lives."

Mountain States Children's Home, where Walter is the director of capital advancement, is a faith based non-profit. Part of their mission statement reads:

Our goal at Mountain States Children's Home is to teach children to be successful in a different way. Our desire is for our children to learn godly character traits such as loving others, treating others as they would like to be treated, dependability, forgiveness, gratefulness, honor, humility, obedience, responsibility, respect, self-control, truthfulness, and wisdom. These are some of the foundational principles of true success in life.

As Walter explains, MSCH has a multipronged approach to target the whole individual, mind, body and spirit, by providing a safe home where all these components are taught.

The MSCH campus includes seven different homes where children live with house parents to provide a loving and caring home environment. Having a mother and father figure in the home provides two different role models with both a male and female perspective.

The whole environment of loving, caring adults—the house parents as well as the counselors and the teachers—help the children feel like they matter. This helps them believe in themselves and opens up the channels of learning academically and healing emotionally.

When a child comes in to the MSCH program they usually have emotional issues and a learning deficit.

The children get one-on-one counseling to help them deal with their emotions. When they come in, they have on average 11-15 areas of concern on the Multidimensional Adolescent Assessment Scale[1]. One year later, 75% of children have between 0-4 areas of concern.

Having a school on campus allows them to focus on catching up in a safe and targeted environment. They learn that they're not dumb. The children tend to achieve an improvement of three or

---

[1] The Multidimensional Adolescent Assessment Scale is a tool for the assessment of the severity of personal and social problems in adolescence. It is composed of 16 subscales relevant to adolescent functioning, including depression; self-esteem; problems with mother, father, or family; personal stress; problems with friends or school; aggression; suicidal thoughts; feelings of guilt; confused thinking; disturbing thoughts; memory loss; and alcohol or drug use.

four academic grade levels per year while they're attending the campus school. Once they catch up with their peers, they transition back to a local school outside the campus.

When they do go back to an outside school, they are confident and prepared, which explains why they have a 100% graduation rate from high school.

It's easy to see why Walter is so excited about what he does. He is making a difference in these children's lives. That's his scorecard.

Two Scorecards

There can be something very satisfying about a scorecard. When we go through school, we receive feedback every time we take a test. Our grade tells us how well we're doing. We learn early on that the scorecard is how to measure success.

After we graduate and go into the world to try our wings, many of us still look for the scorecard that tells us how we're doing. The scorecard no longer comes with A's and B's. Instead, we look at how big our house is, how fancy the car we drive and the size of our bank account. Money and status become the new scorecard for success.

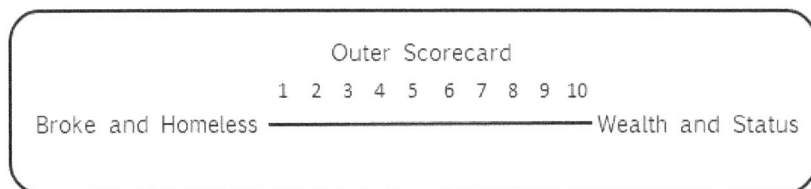

Outer Scorecard

1 2 3 4 5 6 7 8 9 10

Broke and Homeless ——————————— Wealth and Status

Warren Buffett's success has brought him into the orbit of presidents, rubbing shoulders with the richest and most powerful people in the world and his fame as an investor has made him a household name.

This is the outer scorecard. It measures success by our worldly accomplishments and comparing ourselves to others. But the outer scorecard tells only part of the story.

The inner scorecard shows the rest.

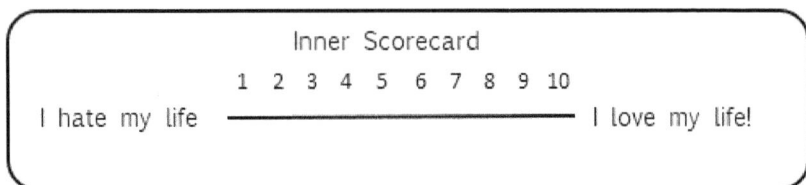

```
                    Inner  Scorecard
            1  2  3  4  5  6  7  8  9  10
I hate my life  ────────────────────────  I love my life!
```

Walter Williams has put more emphasis in his life on the inner scorecard. His primary motivation is love and gratitude. The fact that his life could have turned out quite differently is not lost on him. Aware of how the love that he received from his adoptive parents helped to shape him and his life, his gratitude motivated him to want to help other children who had not been so fortunate.

The outer scorecard was not unimportant to him, but it was secondary, a practical consideration. His goal to continue his college education was less about a desire to deepen his knowledge than it was about being able to earn enough to provide for his family. When the unexpected career change bumped his finances to a new level, he no longer felt the need to continue his education.

Three Components of Success

Becoming successful is a journey and that journey is made up of three main components.

1. A goal. The goal provides a *direction*, the clearer and more specific the goal is the easier it is to hit it.
2. Motivation. The motivation provides the *energy* needed to keep us moving towards our goal.

3. Effort. The effort is the result of a sustained *focus* to keep moving in the right direction.

All three components are needed. You can think of it as driving a car. You can drive for days and go nowhere if you don't have a goal in mind. But let's say you want to drive from San Francisco to New York. Now you have a goal: New York.

To be successful you need two more things: fuel and a map. The fuel is your energy; without it your car won't move. In everyday terms this is your motivation.

You need a map as well. While driving, there will be hundreds of decisions to make: take this highway or that one, get off here or at the next exit, turn left or right. It takes effort to read and follow the map and to keep the car moving in the right direction. To keep making progress towards your goal requires an ongoing effort with a sustained focus and attention.

When you find yourself not making progress towards your goal, it's likely that one of these three is either missing or needs some tweaking.

A Definition for Meaningful Success

Giving a definition of success is like giving a definition for music. We all know what it is, and we can all come up with one, but are you really any wiser if I tell you that music is a composition of sounds in a rhythmic pattern? We care about listening to music because it makes us feel something: sad, excited, or even patriotic. When we do, we resonate with it.

Success is like that too. It's about having a dream and resonating with that dream. We have to feel it or perhaps know it in the depths of our being. If we don't have a personal stake in it, then our success will not give us much satisfaction when we realize our dream. It won't be meaningful.

Meaningful success is about a dream you resonate with, a dream that you feel strong about, or you simply know that it is what you need to do. Your calling. That's the first part. The second part is that your dream should aim to make something better, for you or for someone you care about.

So there it is. Success is your ability to create change. Not any change, but a change that is meaningful to you, that you have a personal stake in, a change that will make things better.

Life is a creative endeavor, or it can be, and it should be. You can *make* it a creative endeavor. You are a living, breathing center of creative energy and it's up to you to give that energy a direction. To find something good and meaningful, something you're willing to sweat and work for, something *hard* and worth doing. Doing hard things makes you grow. It grows your self-esteem, it grows your skills and your grit, and it will make you appreciate your success more.

To borrow a quote from Mark Twain, "The two most important days in your life are the day you were born, and the day you find out why."

All of us have experienced that first day, but only some of us have experienced the second.

It sounds like it's something that happens all of a sudden, and it can seem that way. But in reality, it's something that's inside us for a long time, like a bulb that's underground, waiting for the right time to start growing. We just don't notice it until its first green shoots peek out of the ground. For some of us this happens early, for others late. And for some it never happens.

Purpose. Meaning. A dream, a mission, or even a calling. It's your why. It's why you do what you do. It's why Walter chose to work at the children's home and why Warren, even in his nineties, continues to play the investment game.

Your why is something you discover. It's been inside you from the day you were born, waiting for the right time to show itself. For

Warren it came out early. He knew what he wanted his life to be about.

You may know what it is, or you may not know yet. But it's there.

Your why is what makes your goals meaningful to you. It's one of three essential components that are needed to go from dream to reality. Your why is your fuel. Without it you won't have the energy to move towards your goal.

If you've ever made a half-hearted attempt at creating a new habit, like going to the gym or eating healthier, you know what I mean.

Your why connects you with how you feel about yourself and your life, your inner scorecard.

Exploring What Your Life is About

If you need more clarity on your why, here are some questions you can ask yourself.

Inner Scorecard

1 2 3 4 5 6 7 8 9 10

I hate my life ———————————————— I love my life!

- How would you rate your life on the inner scorecard?

- Was there a period in your life when you would have rated it differently?

- What are the top 3 specific things (good or bad) that influenced your score?

- If you could change anything about your life with a magic wand, what would be your top 3?

- Looking back on your whole life, what are you most grateful for?

- Looking back on your whole life, what do you regret the most?

- Considering your answers to the previous questions, what is most meaningful to you?

Summary

- Success is the result of creating meaningful change in your life.

- Success is a journey which requires three main components to be present: a goal, motivation and sustained effort and focus.

- The outer scorecard measures worldly success. It is dependent on the perceptions and approval of other people.

- The inner scorecard measures spiritual success. It is dependent on how you feel about yourself and your life on a daily basis.

- Discovering your why is what makes your success meaningful.

- Worldly and spiritual success are not mutually exclusive, but usually one of the two dominates your motivation.

- Success, to be meaningful, has to include the inner scorecard, and it has to make something better.

Chapter 2

The Head, the Heart and You

A good head and a good heart are always a formidable combination.

—Nelson Mandela

It was 7:00 a.m. when Jill Taylor woke up on a cold December morning. She had a splitting headache, which was unusual, but she thought exercise might help her feel better. She rolled out of bed and got on her cardio-glider, but her body seemed to feel and respond strangely.

While performing the rhythmic motions on her exercise machine, she had a strange sense of detachment, like she was observing herself, rather than being herself. All the while the piercing pain behind her left eye continued and started to get worse.

Perhaps exercising wasn't such a good idea after all. She climbed off the machine and began to make her way to the bathroom. But walking was no longer the smooth movement she was used to, instead it felt like she had to deliberately move her muscles, resulting in awkward and jerky movements. What had been normal and easy now seemed to cost a lot of effort. What was going on?

Leaning against the wall to maintain her balance, she turned on the shower and was startled by the sound of the water as it hit the tub. It seemed to be extremely loud, which brought on the realization that what was going on went beyond a problem with her physical balance and coordination.

She was searching her brain for answers. She was after all a brain scientist, so if anyone could understand what was going on it would be her. But her brain was no longer cooperating. It simply became quiet. As she searched for answers and information, she instead experienced a growing sense of peace and calm.

No more chatter from her mind. Just an expanding sense of grace. She felt an expansion of her consciousness that soared free and became one with the universe. It felt good. No, it felt better than good; it felt great!

As she describes in her book *My Stroke of Insight*, Dr. Taylor was experiencing the effects of a stroke. The pain behind her left eye was due to a ruptured blood vessel which bled into her brain, slowly eroding her ability to think and control her body. Over the course of several hours, she lost her ability to walk, talk, read, write, and recall any of her life experiences.

She became in a sense like a new-born baby, except that she had an adult body and brain. But it was a brain that had sustained extensive damage.

What fascinates me about her experience is that even though she lost all her skills, all her agency, her essence was still there. Just like we are there when we are born in a baby's body, we have consciousness.

Despite her heavily damaged brain, her consciousness was still there. It was doing what it always does, taking note and experiencing things. And what an experience it was: She experienced herself as a fluid being without borders or limitations, one with the universe. She likened it to Nirvana, feeling a tremendous sense of inner peace and joy.

Consciousness is the part of us that experiences life and it is also in charge of navigating it. It is the captain of our ship as we try to navigate the sea of life.

She, as consciousness, experienced herself and the world through her heart without any interference from her head and it was blissful. There was just one little problem: She couldn't take care of herself.

In the same way that she as a baby had to develop the ability to have control over her body, she had to do it all over again as an adult. She had to decide to take on that task and commit to it, and she did.

Self-Mastery

As consciousness, we have free will. We have choice, and we can decide to create agency—the knowledge and skills we acquire through self-discipline.

That decision to rebuild her brain was not made by her mind which was offline. It was her consciousness that chose to do that. One of its functions is to choose and direct. And in this case, she chose to start rebuilding all the connections in her brain that are necessary to function as a complete human being with a head and a heart.

That took her on an eight-year journey. She had to learn everything all over again, but with one key difference: She did it consciously. And her consciousness had decided not to give up this newfound joy she discovered through the heart. As her left brain began to come back online, she was very aware of its specific functions and programs and chose consciously which programs she wanted to install and kept the rest offline.

This process gave her a whole new appreciation of the ordeal she had gone through. As she slowly rebuilt her left brain, she discovered that she had a choice. The left side of the brain works much like a computer, and she could choose not to include some emotional programs that would lead her to be impatient, critical and unkind with others.

She made a conscious choice not to include patterns of thoughts and emotions that didn't fit who she wanted to be. By taking charge, she forged a new level of freedom, to choose who and how she would be in the world.

Her experience highlights the dual nature that is inside all of us. The head and the heart. Dr. Taylor refers to them as the left and right hemisphere of the brain, or the left and right mind. But she also uses more traditional terms like the heart and heart-consciousness to describe the awareness she experienced through her right hemisphere.

Rather than viewing them as literal parts of the body in charge of this or that, we can look at them as two modes of being that exist inside us simultaneously. Each mode has its own function and sphere of influence, and they both contribute to success in their own way and in different areas of life.

What was unique about Jill's experience is that through her stroke she was given the opportunity to experience in great detail the difference between these two modes of being, and to switch in a matter of hours from primarily running her life with her head, to shifting into her heart.

The subsequent journey of rebuilding the connections in her left hemisphere, consciously and under the supervision of her heart, gave her a lot of insight into the nature of both her head and her heart.

After her stroke she no longer felt separate from others. She felt fluid, connected with everyone and everything, totally at peace and in a state of joy.

That's what we can access through the heart: the experience of life as a spiritual being. This spiritual outlook is hard to communicate because the language of the heart is feeling. It doesn't speak in words, but in feelings, intuitions and knowingness.

In a well-developed heart there is love, both for ourselves and others. It is the source of courage, commitment, enthusiasm and drive and it tells us what is meaningful to us.

But, as Jill discovered through her stroke, the heart by itself is not enough. There are practical matters to attend to. We need to survive, plan for the future, and use our skills to make money.

These practical skills are, by and large, the domain of the head. It remembers the past and plans for the future. It uses language, logic, reason, and linear thinking. But most of all it relies on stories to make sense of the world. When something happens for which it doesn't have a story, it will gladly make one up.

A Model for Success

Success means setting a goal to make things better. The outer and inner scorecard are ways to measure that success. Jill's experience gives us some clues as to how we can harness these two modes of being—the head and the heart—to help us experience success both with our inner and outer scorecard.

Consciousness

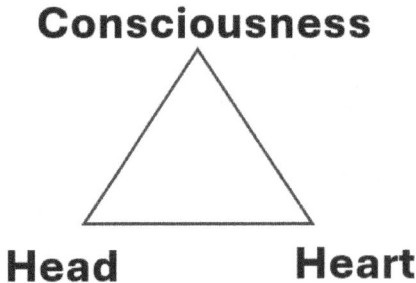

Head   Heart

Figure 2.1 Self-mastery model

- **Consciousness** – Our center of being, the essence of who we are. It is our consciousness that experiences all our thoughts, feelings, and physical sensations. Its role is to experience, learn, make choices and direct our actions and thoughts. Ideally it is in charge of charting the course of our life, but for many people it's not. In the same way that we can use our consciousness to train our body, we can use it to train our mind to use logic and reason, and train our heart to be compassionate, humble and loving.

- **Heart** – One of the two main centers of intelligence and decision making. As a center of intelligence, it perceives and interprets the energy of people and things in our environment. It is a finely tuned instrument that can pick up on people's energy, their moods, intentions and sometimes even their thoughts. Its language is feelings and emotions. We experience love and joy as well as anger, pain and sadness through the heart. It doesn't use logic but uses intuition and feelings to communicate its intelligence. The heart is more closely aligned with spiritual experiences. As a center of decision making, it controls strong motivators like love, desire, fear, anger and courage. It is the driver of commitment. Its roles include assigning value and creating meaning.

- **Head** – The other main center of intelligence and decision making. As a center of intelligence, it processes and stores information much like a computer. It uses logic to run programs. For example: If you see a bear, run. Many of these programs are subconscious. It understands the world through language, stories and models. A model is a story that tells us how something works. If something happens and we don't have a story to explain it, our mind will often make one up on the spot. Its language is words and logic. It performs analytical thinking, creates and executes plans, and uses organization and classification. It sets up the habits that make up all the routine behavior in our day. As a center of decision making, it uses willpower.

We rely on willpower to create new habits and to make ourselves do things that we aren't thrilled about, even though they may be necessary. Its role is to manage the practical aspects of living.

The challenge is that each of these three centers can influence the other two. Sometimes it feels like our head is in control, other times we listen to our heart, or our emotions take over. But self-mastery means that our consciousness is in charge of both the head and the heart.

Not in a way that controls every thought or feeling, but guiding them, like a span of horses in front of a wagon. Like the horses, the head and the heart do most of the hard work, but our consciousness needs to guide and direct them.

This model has been around for centuries in one form or another. Although it is currently out of favor in scientific circles, I think it will come around again because of its practical value.

Success always requires a certain amount of knowledge and self-discipline. This model shows the two main centers of knowledge and discipline inside us, as well as who's in the driver's seat.

The Heart's Role

Most people today consider the heart no more than a pump that keeps our blood circulating. But science has discovered it to be far more than that.

As far back as the 1960s and 70s, John and Beatrice Lacey did groundbreaking research that has shifted our understanding of the heart.

They discovered that the heart has its own intelligence and decision-making powers, which it communicates to the brain through the vagus nerve.

Other researchers built on their findings and discovered that the heart creates and releases hormones and has its own neural network—the heart's brain.

Memory, we believe, lies exclusively in the brain. But research by neurocardiologist Dr. Andrew Armour contradicts this. He discovered that the heart has an elaborate neural network, sometimes called the "little brain", which allows it to act independently from the brain in our head. This little brain—the heart's brain—allows it to learn, remember, and even sense and feel.

Like the brain and the immune system, the heart has a memory. And it freely communicates with the brain, sending it messages through the vagus nerve.

Armour's work in neurocardiology shows that each heartbeat sends signals that are picked up by the brain and other organs. The electromagnetic pulse that accompanies each heartbeat is a source of information that touches every cell in our body. This pulse is so strong that it can be measured more than ten feet away from the body.

Even though science can't penetrate the spiritual secrets of the heart, it does support a much bigger and more independent role of the heart than was previously thought.

In our technology-driven western world there has been a strong push towards relying on logic and reason while downplaying the wisdom of the heart.

Reason has its place of course, but so does the heart.

If you'd like to awaken your heart's potential, here is an exercise I invite you to try.

An Exercise to Awaken the Heart

As an ancient mantra, the word HU has been used throughout history for spiritual upliftment and protection. Practicing this ancient chant each day will awaken your heart. Over time you may find an increasing awareness of your heart's messages, and you may find yourself connecting with it at a deeper level.

To begin, sit or lie down comfortably and close your eyes. Gently place your attention on your heart. To open your heart, think of someone you love or even a pet. Then sing the word HU—pronounced as the name Hugh—in a long-drawn-out breath.

Doing this for ten to fifteen minutes a day will strengthen and awaken your heart.

Why use models?

The city of New York, on their website NYC.gov, has a map gallery with no less than twenty-two different maps of New York. Each map is a model with a different function; to help you find places to get a vaccine, where to find trees, street closures, sidewalk cafés and more.

By highlighting some aspects and eliminating others, the model helps us achieve a task. That's the idea. Every model has a function, and the self-mastery model helps us understand and visualize how we can take charge of our thoughts and emotions, similar to what Jill Taylor did when she rebuilt and retrained her brain's left hemisphere.

Our mind is a model-building machine. These models are our beliefs about how life works, how people work, and how we work. It includes maps of our environment, the laws of physics, and traffic rules to name a few.

We need these models to operate in the world. Some models are pretty good, others are terrible. No model is perfect because the mind has its limitations. Reality is more complex than what our minds can hold, so each model is a necessary simplification that helps us do the best we can.

While these models are both helpful and necessary to navigate life, they also have a downside: They distort our view of the world around us. They create a lens that makes us see reality in a certain way. The lens will highlight certain details and filter out others.

For instance, when I was on vacation in London, I almost stepped in front of an approaching car. The model in my head, which "knew" where the cars were—or were supposed to be—only looked for cars driving on the right side of the road and missed all the cars driving on the left.

In this book I introduce several models. The main reason is that our minds work with models whether we like it or not. Our understanding of reality is largely based on the models we hold in our head. Good models excel because they're useful and they help us make good decisions. They allow us to better navigate to the future we want.

The flip side is that every model has its flaws. It's a simplified version of reality, so you can always run into a situation where the model doesn't work.

How Models Create Views of Reality

A chair is a solid object. You can sit on it, kick it, or throw it against a wall, it's still solid. And yet, science tells us it is mostly empty space.

If you did not damage the chair, you might try sitting down on it, and it would appear you are motionless. If you zoom out far enough though, you are actually hurtling through space at 67,000 miles per hour, making your way around the sun while simultaneously traveling over 1,000 miles per hour while revolving around Earth's axis.

Reality is vast and complex. Sometimes we need to look at it with a different lens, to understand a different aspect of it. You are standing still and you're hurtling through space. The chair is a solid object and it's mostly made up of empty space. Its atoms give it form and shape and these same atoms are nothing but energy.

On the face of it, these views may seem incompatible, but as science shows us, they are all true simultaneously. It depends on which lens we're using.

When Oppenheimer was working on the Manhattan project he needed to view reality through the lens of the atom as an equivalent of energy. Einstein's $E = MC^2$ was the view that guided Oppenheimer and his band of scientists, and it eventually led to the first nuclear bomb.

Neil Armstrong's journey to the moon required a lens that sees the Earth as a ball hurtling through space, with the moon as a different ball circling around it.

To better understand reality, we need multiple models and views. Sometimes these views appear to be in conflict, and we feel the need to choose one. More often than not this is a case of the either-or fallacy: We believe two views are in conflict while in reality they complement each other.

Different models and views provide different lenses that can help us solve different problems. There is no single view that covers everything. You can think of these views as providing depth. We have two eyes. Our brain deftly combines the images of both eyes into a single image with depth. Using multiple models and views brings greater depth and understanding of the terrain we need to cover to successfully move from where we are today to where we want to be in the future.

Summary

- The self-mastery model shows the two main components we need to master for success: the head and the heart.

- The head represents our physical, material nature. It helps us navigate the physical world, and it strongly corresponds with the outer scorecard.

- The heart is aligned with our spiritual nature, and it strongly contributes to the score on our inner scorecard.

- Our mind relies on models and stories to understand reality. Every model is a simplification of reality with a specific purpose. No model is perfect, but good models help us make good decisions.

- Each model creates a lens that lets us view some aspect of reality in more detail, while filtering out other aspects.

- When two viewpoints appear to be in conflict because they are different, they often provide two valid and complementary views of reality.

Chapter 3

The Key to Mastery and Excellence

*There is a powerful driving force inside every human being that,
once unleashed, can make any vision, dream, or desire a reality.*
—Anthony Robbins

Was it coincidence or was it fate?

When Richard turned on the television, he saw the twenty-five-year-old Virginia Ruzici from Romania who received a forty-thousand-dollar check for winning a tennis tournament.

"Not bad for four days' work," the announcer quipped.

Richard couldn't believe what he saw. That was more money than he made in a year. The way Richard tells it, he read the paper the next day and when it confirmed what he had seen on TV, he decided right there and then to have two more kids and put them in tennis.

The real story, as he shares it in his book *Black and White: The Way I See It*, shows there was a bit more to it.

He definitely was fascinated with the idea. His thoughts kept going back to this dream of having two girls and turning them into tennis champions. It was a decision that once he made it, would take his life—and that of his whole family—into a completely different direction. But how to know if it was the right thing to do? He listened to his heart.

Whenever he had a major decision to make, he had a way to tune into his heart at a deeper level. He would gaze at the night sky, looking for a sign. That night he received the sign he was looking for.

As he looked at the sky he saw a bright star that seemed set apart from the rest. He saw the star as a sign that his children would be set apart from the other tennis players. And not because they were African Americans, but because they would dominate the game.

After this he fell asleep in the grass and dreamed of his two daughters. When raindrops woke him, he could still hear their voices calling him Daddy. In that moment he had no more doubt: he was going to have two daughters!

The heart connects us to our divine nature. Through dreams, intuition and sometimes just knowing. But we need to quiet our mind and emotions to hear it. Richard knew that. His way of quieting everything else was to look at the night sky. And the answer came. His heart knew, he could feel it in his soul.

It's something few of us know and appreciate: The heart makes decisions. We've been taught that all decision making is done by the brain. Fortunately, that is not the case. The heart has a way of helping us make long-term and life-changing decisions, even if they don't always make sense. The key is to listen.

The second key might be not to listen to the voice in our head which is always on hand to talk us out of it. Richard had this voice too, and it gave him all the reasons why it couldn't work. After all, he didn't know a thing about tennis. And how was he going to teach his kids a game he himself didn't know how to play? And there was of course his wife, who would have to agree to having two more kids.

He had never really liked this game that was predominantly played by white people, and yet, his heart had settled on it. Rather than letting his mind talk him out of it, he gave it a job to do.

He wrote a detailed seventy-five-page plan, to educate and train himself, his wife, and his daughters-to-be. All of this more than two years before his daughters were born.

Was it a crazy idea? Almost anyone would have thought so, but he never let that bother him. He approached it the same way he had learned to run his own business, with absolute faith and confidence that he would be able to figure it out.

Plan Your Work and Work Your Plan

Once he had planned his work, it was time to work his plan and put the first step of his plan into action: learning how to play tennis.

His curiosity and research into tennis soon began to consume him. As the owner of a security company, he could do most of his work at night and he spent all the rest of his time learning more about the game.

He immersed himself in the game with books, videos and the help of an old tennis teacher nicknamed Old Whiskey, because he took his payments for teaching in whiskey. He sought out experts in the National Junior Tennis League and the United States Tennis Association. He was like a sponge soaking up all the knowledge, while at the same time working on his tennis skills.

But there was one thing he found troubling, and that was the proper way to position his feet. All the experts agreed that a closed stance was the way to go, but he thought an open stance would be better. So he practiced it over and over until he perfected it.

The training program he embarked on was an eclectic mix. Besides practicing and playing tennis, it included playing baseball and basketball to enhance his ability to see and track the ball, while throwing the ball helped him with his serve. To improve his balance, he took dancing lessons. He even revisited boxing to help him with his footwork and hand movements.

That's what it looks like when you go from making a commitment to becoming obsessed. Obsession gives you a focus that is impossible to achieve without it. It's this laser-like focus that allows you to pour your heart into this ONE thing. With this focus, discipline becomes easy, and excellence is the natural result.

A couple of months after beginning his journey into all things tennis, Richard started playing on one of the public tennis courts. He was no match for his opponent—The Colonel—who beat him in two straight sets. Richard wasn't able to win a single game, but he was good-natured about it. He was just beginning to learn.

After three more months of intense practice, he was ready to see if all his work had any bearing on the real world. He had stopped playing at the public courts to focus on his practice. Now he went back to the same tennis court and faced the opponent who had given him such a sound beating. It appeared his hard work had paid off. This time he turned the tables on The Colonel, beating him 6–0, 6–0.

The Key to Mastery

Figure 3.1

The key to mastery and excellence is commitment and self-discipline, but there is a catch. Commitment and self-discipline are easy when we make the commitment from the heart. But the heart resists force in any way. When we try to force ourselves, with reasons that appeal to our head, we can make a commitment, but it will be from our head.

A commitment from the head has a few disadvantages: 1. When obstacles arise, they easily throw us off. 2. Our heart is not in it, and it shows. 3. Willpower will get us out the door, but willpower is limited. It rarely has the staying power to get us to the finish line.

Some people would argue a commitment made with the head is not a commitment at all, because so often we change our mind and renege on the responsibility we have committed to.

How is a commitment from the heart different? It does not depend on willpower; it depends on heart-power, which is love. Even things that are hard, like learning to play an instrument, can be enjoyable if our heart has committed to it. When obstacles come up, they are faced and when our heart is in it, we have the energy to overcome them.

That's why a large commitment, like the one Richard and his wife Oracene made, required a heart-centered decision. The self-discipline and love that over time created the mastery of the game that resulted in Venus and Serena ranking as #1 and #2 in the world was powered by the heart.

Moving to Compton

Six years later Richard put the next, and frankly the craziest part of his plan into motion. By this time Venus and Serena had been born and were almost two and three years old. They were living in Long Beach, a haven of tranquility, close to the beach.

Richard changed all that. Over the objections of his wife, he moved the whole family from Long Beach to Compton.

The greater Los Angeles area had good parts and bad parts. And then there was Compton. Only eleven miles north of where they used to live, it could best be described as a war zone. The city was controlled by gangs. Drugs and gang violence were the order of the day, claiming almost fourteen hundred lives in a twenty-year span.

What led him to Compton was his belief that the greatest champions came out of the ghetto. He decided that moving there would make his girls tough and help them develop a fighter's mentality.

It shows the level of commitment he had to his dream, sure. But was it wise? When commitment turns into an obsession, it can lead to great achievements, but it can also make us lose perspective and lead to making unbalanced and unwise decisions.

He wanted his girls to use the public tennis courts to practice, and the gangs used those courts to conduct their "business." When he kindly requested them to move and conduct their business elsewhere, they ignored him. He wanted the courts, and they did not want to give them up. This was the setup for an ongoing power struggle between Richard and the gang members.

In the end Richard prevailed and was able to use the public tennis courts with his girls. But not before he was beaten up badly, losing a number of his teeth.

Now that the tennis courts were his to use, Richard could move on to the next part of his plan: teaching the girls.

Teaching the Girls

To become champions, the girls would need to learn to play tennis. Richard's plan provided for this: He and his wife became their tennis coaches.

Every day, Richard would load the whole family into his Volkswagen minibus and drive them to one of the public tennis courts to practice. Even when not on the court, they would watch tennis matches on TV and on video, analyzing what was happening and why. Tennis became a family affair, and perhaps more accurately, a family obsession.

But tennis wasn't all that the girls were learning. Richard had a philosophy about success, and he wanted to train the girls not just in tennis, but in adopting the success principles that had served him well throughout his life.

Successful people recognize how things work. They are able to consciously or subconsciously understand the principles that lead to success and have learned to apply them in their life.

Most successful people have created their own guide to success. They have boiled it down to certain key principles and achieved success by applying these principles in their life.

Richard used what he calls *The Williams Life Triangle*. His triangle focuses on the heart qualities of faith, confidence, courage and commitment.

But having planned for two of his kids to become tennis champions, he obviously also understands the importance of planning, which is the domain of the head.

That's why he had Venus and Serena write out what they were committing to, from when they were little. He wanted them to get into the habit of writing down their goals and what steps they would take to make them come true.

He'd always try to find some time to help them write down what they planned to accomplish that week. It helped them to focus on their commitments and to measure their success.

He taught his kids to plan and then reinforced the habit with his favorite maxim: "If you fail to plan you plan to fail."

While planning requires logic and analysis, which is what our head excels at, implementing the plan is where the heart qualities in Richard's life triangle come in.

First is commitment, which means caring. Do you care enough to follow through and do the things that need doing to get to your goal?

Second is courage or overcoming fear. Do you have the fortitude to do the things that need doing, in the face of real or perceived danger?

Third is confidence, which centers on believing. It is the can-do spirit, the belief that you will succeed and that you have what it takes to overcome the obstacles that you find in your way.

And at the center he puts faith. While confidence means we trust in our own abilities, faith is placing trust in a higher power, which in Richard's life takes center stage.

These heart qualities are hard to measure, but they're every bit as real and necessary as the goal and the plan. They represent different aspects of the inner strength that is needed to keep you moving forward. You don't get them from reading a book; you have to grow them. Inner strength comes from facing ourselves. We grow from doing, not from reading. And we grow as much— and often more—from failing as we do from being successful.

Richard's philosophy about raising children was to teach them success skills, and to allow them to fail. He felt that failure is an integral part of learning, and he wasn't afraid to let his girls make mistakes.

Learning Commitment

At fourteen, Venus was going to play her first professional tournament in Oakland. Richard noticed that her tennis dress was still sitting on top of the TV, so he asked her if she had everything. Oh yes, she was excited and ready to go, and sure she had everything. He asked her two more times before they left, and each time Venus was sure she had everything.

So they left the hotel room with Venus's tennis dress still on the TV.

When she arrived at the tennis court and realized she was missing her tennis outfit, she started crying, especially after finding out Richard had known they left the room without it.

When she asked him if he knew, he admitted that he did. She couldn't understand why he didn't say anything and had let her leave without her outfit. But as Richard pointed out to her, it wasn't his responsibility, it was hers.

It was a teachable moment, and Richard took full advantage of it. He was willing to allow her to fail, to make her own mistakes, so she could learn from them.

Richard understood that commitment is like a muscle, and if you want to strengthen it you need to work it. Children don't learn to take responsibility if everything is done for them. Allowing them to fail is part of the process. Failure is instructive, it teaches us to take responsibility.

Apparently Venus took the lesson to heart, because from that day forward she started using a checklist before every match.

Some people would say it was cruel of him to consciously let her fail. But isn't that what parents are supposed to do? To let their kids fail, as long as it is safe to do so? We learn the lesson of responsibility so much quicker and better that way.

Commitment means taking responsibility and the sooner we learn to take responsibility for our life the better.

Fear, Courage, Confidence and Acting As If

Some of us are naturally more confident than others. Our early upbringing and the role models we had play a role in this. We absorb both the overt and more subtle messages from our parents—and sometimes siblings, teachers and friends too—that can push us in the direction of more or less confidence.

So what do we do if we have no confidence in our own abilities? How can we gain courage and confidence when all we have is fear or a negative self-image?

There's a little-known principle called the as-if principle. By acting as if we have courage, we actually become courageous. Acting as if we have confidence is also the first step to becoming confident. We can bring those traits we desire into the present, by acting as if we are what we want to become.

We learn by doing, and the first step is to act as if we already are confident, courageous and committed.

It is a simple tool we can use to build strength in the heart when it is still lacking.

Another way to build these heart qualities is by giving our mind overt messages and keep repeating them. Richard helped the girls build a confident mindset by giving them positive messages over and over.

He would write out these empowering messages, or better yet, he'd let the girls write them out on a big piece of paper. Then he'd hang up the paper all around the tennis court. He really put a lot of effort into it, because he realized how important it was for the girls to be confident and believe in themselves.

It's a simple fact that most of us will adopt a belief if it is repeated to us often enough. Repetition is a simple tool, and he was using it to build a positive mindset for the girls. Especially at that age the girls' minds were like sponges; they soaked up everything he put into them. And he made sure they believed they were championship material.

Building the girls' mindset was a key element of the plan, and he was careful not to let others interfere with it.

During the filming of an ABC News segment in 1995 Venus was being interviewed.

Interviewer: "Do you think you can beat her?"
Venus: "I know I can beat her."
Interviewer: "You know you can beat her?"
Venus smiles and nods.
Interviewer: "Very confident."
Venus: "I'm very confident."
Interviewer: "You say it so easily. Why?"

Venus: "Cause I believe it."
Richard: "Alright, cut right there if you don't mind. And let me tell you why. What she said, she said it with so much confidence the first time but you keep going on and on. You have to understand that you're dealing with an immature fourteen-year-old child. And this child gonna be out there playing when your old ass and me gonna be in the grave. When she says something we done told you what's happening. You're dealing with a little black kid and let her be a kid. She answered with a lot of confidence, leave that alone!"

He didn't want the reporter to start planting doubts in her mind. He was protective of them, not only physically, but also mentally. The mindset he had been nurturing was exceptional and precious, and he knew it.

That mindset served them well when they turned pro and began playing tournaments. They had the skills, and they believed in themselves. It took them several years, but in 2002 Venus was able to reach the #1 ranking in women's tennis. A few months later Serena overtook her and claimed the #1 spot.

His obsession had produced two tennis stars that ended up dominating women's tennis.

Richard had predicted it. He had trained and prepared them for it. And they did it.

Summary

- Success means mastery. We have to master some aspect of the game of life, and the way to master it is by making a commitment.

- Not all decisions are made with our head. The heart also makes decisions. It can overcome fear, inspire confidence and help to motivate us. True commitment is a decision of the heart.

- Mastery is always the result of a combined effort of the head and the heart. An example is to plan your work and work your plan. While planning is the domain of the head, working your plan requires a decision of the heart.

- Commitments come in different shapes and sizes. The deepest, most encompassing form of commitment is obsession. While commitment means we care, obsession means we care enough to completely immerse ourselves and change into the person we need to become to be successful.

- While we can commit to multiple goals, obsession is a choice of the heart to pursue a single goal. If we have an obsession, it will determine the direction of our life.

- Obsession can lead to great achievements, but it is also a state that can easily lead to an unbalanced life and unwise decisions. The challenge is to maintain a level of balance.

Chapter 4

The Power of Principles

Everything that exists in your life does so because of two things: something you did or something you didn't do.

—Albert Einstein

One of Einstein's most famous quotes is that "God doesn't play dice with the universe." He was convinced that we live in an ordered universe, and that we, through our own efforts, can increase our understanding of that order. In other words, if we try, we can figure out how things work.

Isaac Newton, a few centuries earlier, came to the same conclusion. As a natural philosopher—they weren't yet known as scientists, that would come later—he was the first to unravel the natural laws[2] that control the movement of objects, by formulating the three laws of motion.

Newton truly had a brilliant mind. How many people could study some mathematical texts on their own and then invent calculus? His ability to grasp principles and describe them, as well as how they work mathematically, was extraordinary.

But although few people would dispute his genius, he did have his challenges.

---

[2] Natural law – a system of law that is determined by nature and is thus universal.

Newton's strengths and weaknesses follow a pattern that is not altogether uncommon. With his talent for rational, scientific thought he created a masterpiece when he wrote *Mathematical Principles of Natural Philosophy*, better known as the *Principia*—which is Latin for principles. In it he laid out why the heavenly bodies move the way they do: because of the law of gravity. He wasn't the first to observe gravity, but he was able to discover the formulas that explained the movements of objects as well as planets.

As brilliant as he was when using his mind to unravel the laws of the universe, the rest of him was decidedly less brilliant. Given to strange experiments, he once inserted a needle that was ordinarily used for sewing leather into his eye socket and rubbed it around as far as he could to see what would happen. He miraculously didn't lose his eye or his eyesight.

On top of that he was insecure, petty, and easily provoked into anger to the point of being unhinged. His deep insecurities left him extremely anxious when he published his work, and he would fly into an uncontrolled rage when other scientists disagreed with him.

Rivalries with other scientists quickly turned into full-blown battles that went on for years. In his pettiness he spent time removing any references to Robert Hooke from a revised edition of *Principia*, because he and Hooke had gotten embroiled in a conflict that didn't end until Hooke died.

He also got into a tiff with John Flamsteed. As Royal Astronomer he owned a large set of data that Newton wanted access to for an updated version of his *Principia*. When Flamsteed didn't provide the data to him as fast as Newton wanted, he used his power as president of the Royal Society to get hold of it and tried to publish the data. Flamsteed had to get a court order to get the data back and keep it from being published without his consent.

After his *Principia* with mathematical proofs began to circulate, Newton's star began to rise. Over time his insights were recognized—by the few who could understand the way he had written it down—and voila. His success on the outer scorecard could hardly be higher. At the end of his life he had become Sir Isaac Newton, Master of the Mint and President of the Royal Society. He had wealth, power and status. He was honored with a state funeral, the first time ever, for someone whose accomplishments lay in the realm of knowledge and the mind.

But his score on the inner scorecard hardly registered. He never married. He suffered a nervous breakdown at least twice, and he was embroiled in conflicts with other scientists for most of his life. He never found the spiritual principles that are locked in the heart.

Not for lack of trying by the way. This side of Newton is not as well known, but he was an avid alchemist. Newton grasped the mechanical nature of the universe and used his mathematical skills to describe how the mechanical side of things worked. But he could not believe in nature without spirit. Alchemists did more than try to turn base metals into gold; they tried to understand the spiritual nature of reality, to find the life force that runs everything.

Today we don't think twice about it, but in his day proposing gravity as an invisible force was controversial. You'd think that everyone immediately lined up behind him, but that was hardly the case. Many of his contemporaries scoffed at it. Gottfried Leibniz, a bit of a genius himself, had initially been one of his admirers, but later turned against him, mocking the idea of gravitation.

But reason compelled Newton to assume it exists. It was simple cause and effect. Like magnetism and electricity, gravity is an invisible force we don't fully understand, but we can observe its effects.

He couldn't explain why gravity exists, which is still true today, but based on his observations he knew it had to exist.

Newton really started something. By outlining the principles that underly the way objects move, he started a movement. He recognized there was order in the universe, and he began to map that order. Generations of scientists have continued his work of finding these principles.

Although these principles don't tell us the *why* of the universe, they do help us understand better *how* it all works.

These principles are around us all the time. They are baked into the fabric of the universe, but it takes a special ability to recognize them.

Newton had that ability.

But for all the brilliance of his mind, Newton only had half the picture. He started mapping the principles that create order in the physical universe, but he never found the spiritual principles that are locked inside the heart. He had an open mind, but he wasn't able to open his heart.

The heart doesn't operate using logic and reason; it operates on love.

While today's Western culture readily recognizes the principles that science has uncovered, it is still largely in the dark about the spiritual principles that can be discovered through the heart.

The heart tracks the order of the universe in its own way too. Spiritual principles are the domain of the heart, but these principles are easily overlooked unless we learn to pay attention to the messages coming from our heart.

The Cost of Winning at All Costs

Serena was the underdog. She was the younger sister, always in Venus's shadow, and she desperately wanted to prove herself. She wanted to win.

As a young girl she admits to sometimes having taken the low road while playing tennis. That meant winning by any means possible, including cheating. When she was playing her older sister, who at that time simply had a better game than she did, she nevertheless tried to beat her by cheating. She called balls out when they were in, and Venus never corrected her. She simply let her little sis get away with it.

In her book *On The Line*, Serena tells the story of how she once cheated to win at tennis—as a seven-year-old—while playing in the Domino's Pizza League. The girls were supposed to keep score themselves and then report the outcome after they were done. Anne was up 5 – 2, but for a moment lost track of the score and asked Serena what the score was.

Serena brazenly asserted that the score was 5 – 2 in *her* favor, and for some reason Anne bought it. But not for long. When Anne remembered that she had been the one up by three games she confronted Serena, but Serena forcefully pronounced she was wrong and continued to assert herself until Anne let it go.

After that, Anne ended up battling back to a 5 – 5 score, so if the match had been fair, she really would have won the set. But Serena ended up taking the next two games and "won" the set 7 – 5.

Yes, it's possible to get what we want by distorting the truth, but there are consequences.

While scientists like Newton tried to push back the fog of ignorance and figure out the rules by which our physical world operates, religions try to teach us the spiritual rules. Most religions teach that there is some form of divine justice. For instance, in the Christian Bible it says that what a man sows he will also reap.

Buddhism and Hinduism know this principle as karma. What we put out into the world will come back to us. Newton discovered the physical counterpart to this principle in his third law of motion: For every action, there is an equal and opposite reaction.

The problem in recognizing this principle—for most of us—is the time that passes between our initial action and the moment life returns it to us.

Serena did face the karma she created when she cheated Anne out of a deserved win, but it was many years later. In 2004 she played in the U.S. Open tournament and faced Jennifer Capriati in the quarterfinals. For some reason, the umpire scored a point that had clearly been Serena's for Jennifer. Serena complained as forcefully and respectfully as she could with the umpire, to no avail. The point went to Jennifer.

The "lost" point messed with her head. It broke her concentration, and Jennifer ended up breaking her serve to go up 1 – 0 in the third set. That got Serena even more upset, feeling that that single bad call by the umpire came back to bite her, setting a negative tone for the rest of the match.

What had come back to bite her was her karma from many years ago, but she of course didn't see it that way. As they continued to play, several calls by the umpire were just plain wrong. Serena ended up mouthing off to the umpire while she and Jennifer changed sides, and said, "I can't believe you would sabotage me like that."

It's likely that Anne thought the same thing when Serena brazenly inverted the score and took Anne's lead as her own, who knows? But it's no stretch to imagine that Serena's actions might have messed with Anne's head. Upset, confused, why would this other girl do something like that? It wasn't fair.

Exactly the way Serena was feeling during her game with Jennifer. Why would the umpire do something like that? It wasn't fair. And yet it was, because karma is divine justice. What we sow, we reap.

The symmetry between the matches is hard to miss. In their childhood match Anne fought back and almost overcame the false lead Serena had created for herself. Almost. But then she still lost. Serena likewise got her hopes up in the game with Jennifer, fighting back despite the bad calls by the umpire, getting her hopes up. But then she lost the match that would have likely been hers, if the refereeing had been fair.

Unlike Newton's laws of motion, which can be measured and validated, there is no way to prove that karma was at play here. Perhaps it was a coincidence, who's to say? Spiritual principles are easy to deny and discount—as easy as it was for Serena to deny Anne's lead and claim it as her own. That's how it is when we look at karma from a mental perspective. It's only by looking at it with the heart that we can perceive the truth of it. Laws of physics can be validated with our head. Spiritual laws[3] require validation with the heart.

The Rules of the Game

Life doesn't come with an instruction manual, so it's up to each of us to create our own. Universal principles are the closest thing we can find that resembles an instruction manual. They represent the rules of the game. They tell us how life works.

Newton's principles have stood the test of time. They allowed us to send men to the moon. It would not have been possible without the principles he discovered.

That's what principles allow us to do—they give us the freedom to forge our own path, even to the moon and back.

Karma is the spiritual law that teaches personal responsibility—it is our own thoughts, feelings, and actions that are responsible for how our life turns out.

As a spiritual principle, it runs counter to a perception that's so common in society today—that we are victims who are unfairly treated through no fault of our own. Serena's example is nothing special, you probably have at least one example where you felt you were treated unfairly too. You know you didn't deserve it, and yet it happened.

---

[3] Spiritual law – a divine, universal principle that applies to all people and situations, regardless of time and place.

Self-responsibility can be hard to swallow. It's so much easier to point the finger of blame to someone else. But that's what karma is: the principle of self-responsibility.

How to Find the True Causes for What Is Wrong in Your Life

Here's a little trick I learned that has been incredibly helpful. By taking the principle of karma or self-responsibility up a notch, I turned it into a self-fulfilling prophecy that works to my benefit.

When I was writing computer code there were numerous times when I had written a program, ran it through the compiler—a software program that translates a programming language into computer instructions—and the compiler would tell me I made a mistake. Syntax is very strict when you write code. Many times, I would look at the code and everything looked good to me.

Still, the compiler disagreed.

In those cases, I would hear myself mutter, *It doesn't make any sense.* And I would double my efforts to look for the error, but no dice. I couldn't find it. The reason was that I had settled on the belief that it didn't make any sense, which was a different way of saying that the compiler was wrong. Eventually, I learned a trick to help me find the problem. As soon as I would catch myself saying or thinking *It doesn't make any sense*, I would override my thinking and say, *There's a logical explanation here, I just haven't found it yet.* By making this switch in my thinking I opened up my mind, and all of a sudden, I could see what had been hidden before: the problem in the code.

This little quirk of the mind—it doesn't like to be wrong, so it quietly alters our perception—isn't limited to computer programming. Psychologists call it the confirmation bias, and it all too often leads to a self-fulfilling prophecy. Our mind filters out information that disagrees with our current beliefs. It also actively selects information that agrees with our beliefs.

It's a tricky feature that can keep you stuck in a false belief for a long time, but once you're aware of it, you can use it to your advantage.

So here is the key.

You start with the assumption that *everything* in your life is there because you have caused it to be there. Everything is the result of a choice you've made. It may be because of a persistent thought or belief, or something you have done, even a very long time ago.

In other words, you accept full responsibility for every condition in your life. You can call it karma, divine justice, or anything else, but you can't call it somebody else's fault, *even if it clearly is.*

If you do this, your mind miraculously opens up to seeing things that were completely invisible before.

This shift in belief is powerful, because it shifts your perception. Everything in your life becomes feedback. You can start looking at which thoughts, attitudes, beliefs, or past actions may have contributed to the current condition.

It's a simple thing, but if you take this approach and truly see yourself as 100% responsible for every aspect of your life, you will be amazed at what you discover.

As your perception shifts, you will gain a level of control and agency which will give you an edge. You will discover very quickly which actions, habits, and beliefs are for your benefit and which are not.

Summary

- The universe has order, and we can better understand that order through principles. Success depends on the correct understanding of those principles.

- The principles we discover with our mind are worldly principles. They help us understand the laws of the physical universe through logic and reason, and they help us to plan, organize and be efficient. They also are the foundation for some of the inventions that make life more enjoyable and give us more freedom, like TVs, cars, airplanes and computers.

- The principles we discover with the heart are spiritual principles. They help us discover the difference between right and wrong, and how to live a more joyful, fulfilling, and meaningful life. These principles are the foundation for understanding both human and divine justice.

- Karma is the spiritual principle that teaches responsibility. Our thoughts, feelings and actions go out into the world and then come back to us. What we sow, we reap.

- Insight into both worldly and spiritual laws and principles gives us more freedom. They help us make better choices, because we better understand what those choices will lead to.

- Natural laws can be measured and validated using our head. Spiritual laws are discovered and validated through the heart.

The Integrity Code

Part Two

Journey of the Heart

Life is not random, but
a steady progression of
the heart from
an immature state to
a more mature one.

Chapter 5

The Maturity Principle

As you grow older, you stand for more and fall for less.

—Anonymous

Philip Zimbardo was born in the 1930s and grew up in the South Bronx. It was a tough place, and it shaped him.

As he explains in the book *The Lucifer Effect*, as a kid growing up there, gangs were a fact of life. So he developed street smarts. He figured out who had power that could be used either for or against him, and which people to avoid and with whom to ingratiate himself.

To become part of the gang he went through an initiation process, which meant he had to steal, fight and intimidate girls and Jewish kids.

In that environment none of it was considered bad or evil. He was simply falling in line with the norms of the gang and following the gang leader.

The cops, on the other hand, were the enemy and not to be trusted. They would come and confiscate the broomstick "bat" and rubber ball they were using to play stickball in the streets. So they got smart and hid their broomstick when the police approached.

One time, the cops asked Philip where they had hidden their ball and broomstick, but he wouldn't talk.

One cop said he would arrest him and pushed him into the squad car, smashing his head against the door. It made him wary of people in uniform ever since, assuming they were not to be trusted unless proven otherwise.

Philip went on to college and became a researcher and professor in the field of social psychology at Stanford University.

His experience of growing up in the ghetto fostered a deep curiosity into the nature of good and evil, and what forces play into a person becoming good or bad.

He assumed that the roles we take on and the systems we are a part of have a larger influence on our behavior than most of us realize, and he created an experiment to test his assumption.

The experiment—later dubbed the Stanford Prison Experiment—took twenty-four young men, then randomly assigned half of them to the prisoner role and the other half to the guard role.

From the start the intention was to maximize the influence of the role and minimize individuality of the participants. To that end prisoners were given uniforms with a number, front and back, for identification and instructed only to refer to other prisoners by number. They also made them wear a nylon stocking to cover their hair, because it promoted greater anonymity among the prisoners.

The guards were outfitted with equally role appropriate uniforms, reflecting sunglasses that would hide their eyes, whistles, handcuffs and billy clubs.

That this prison experiment would soon go off the rails should have been no surprise, given that the "guards" were given minimal training and were counseled to create a psychological atmosphere that would capture some of the essential features found in many prisons.

Although they weren't allowed to physically abuse the prisoners, they were actively encouraged to be tough. Some of the guards weren't really getting into the role. They were taken aside and told that their individual style had been a little too soft and that they were trying to set up the stereotypical guard.

They were told to be tough, and that meant to use their power to dominate the prisoners. Some got into this more than others.

As Zimbardo describes, there were three distinct behaviors that emerged among the guards.

One group of guards enjoyed the power that was cast upon them and turned evil[4] by finding creative ways to demean and hurt the prisoners. The guards in the second group played their role well. They were tough and demanding, but were not abusive, although there was little regard for the hardships of the men in the prisoner role. The third group showed more compassion. Zimbardo classified them as "good guards" because they would do little things for the prisoners, like giving one an apple and another a cigarette. They didn't let the role they were playing override their basic humanity.

Zimbardo notes that none of the personality tests they administered to the test subjects were able to predict which guards would turn evil, which played it strictly by the rules and which were willing to be kind.

Although his experiment did make the point that the roles we take on and the systems we participate in exert a strong influence on our behavior, not everyone was equally affected by these forces.

A question not clearly answered by the experiment and Zimbardo's subsequent reflections on it is this: If personality tests could not predict why some guards became evil, and others remained good, then what was responsible for the difference in behavior?

---

4 The definition of evil used by Zimbardo: Evil consists in intentionally behaving in ways that harm, abuse, demean, dehumanize, or destroy innocent others, or using one's authority and systemic power to encourage or permit others to do so on your behalf.

A Theory of Learning

Jean Piaget discovered that children learn things in a specific order. If you show a child a ball of clay, and you flatten the ball of clay, children up to the age of eight will think that now there is more clay, because it's bigger. At eight years old 75% of children recognize the principle of conservation of matter—it's the same amount of clay. It takes another year or two before 75% of children recognize that not only is it the same amount of clay, it also is the same weight—conservation of weight. And only around age twelve do 75% of children realize that it's the same volume as well—conservation of volume.

Although the timing of these insights can vary based on background and experience, the order stays the same. First we learn conservation of matter, then weight, and finally volume.

He's saying that as our brain and thinking develops, there is a natural progression. We grasp this view intuitively. If we look at our physical skills there is a similar progression—we have to learn to crawl before we can walk and walk before we can run. Although different children can start to crawl, walk and run at different ages, they all follow the same progression. We have to master one skill before we can tackle a new skill that depends on the skill we've learned before.

The maturity principle is based on the observation that maturity in its different aspects always follows a predictable order. We go through stages, as we make our way from an immature state to a more mature one.

Developmental psychologists Jean Piaget and Maria Montessori championed this principle, each in their own way. They used it to guide how children learn as they make their way through school. Other psychologists, focusing more on personality traits, discovered that—like a good wine—our personality gets better as we age. We tend to become more conscientious, confident, caring, and calm as we get older.

The maturity principle shows up in different areas of our life and shows that experience at any age leads to changes in physical and cognitive abilities and personality as well.

Maturity of the Heart

The prison guards in the Stanford Prison Experiment didn't all react the same way to the pressures put on them by the roles they were asked to step into. The way they reacted was simply another aspect of the maturity principle: a maturity not measured by age, personality or cognitive abilities, but by the state of their heart.

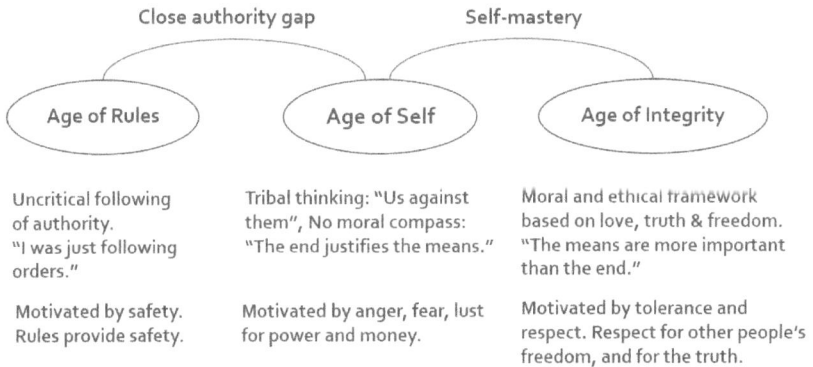

	Close authority gap		Self-mastery	
Age of Rules		**Age of Self**		**Age of Integrity**
Uncritical following of authority. "I was just following orders."		Tribal thinking: "Us against them", No moral compass: "The end justifies the means."		Moral and ethical framework based on love, truth & freedom. "The means are more important than the end."
Motivated by safety. Rules provide safety.		Motivated by anger, fear, lust for power and money.		Motivated by tolerance and respect. Respect for other people's freedom, and for the truth.

Figure 5.1

As we learn and grow, the heart goes through three distinct stages.

The Age of Rules

The heart's first stage is characterized by learning the rules. As a child our first teachers and source of authority are our parents and sometimes older siblings. Children view life through a lens of authority which provides structure and security.

In Zimbardo's experiment these were the guards that were simply doing their job, following the rules and making sure the inmates followed the rules.

It's the case of being the thermometer instead of the thermostat. We go along with the strongest influence in our environment. If that is a positive influence it shapes us and our life in a positive way, if it's negative then it shapes us in a more negative direction.

When we live in a society where the rules are just, life is mostly good. But these rules can change over time. When the rules become unjust, as was the case in the ghetto where Zimbardo grew up, life becomes harsh.

At this level of maturity there is no critical thinking, no personal assessment of the rules as good or bad. We allow an outside authority to define the rules, and we follow them.

This outer authority can be any authority figure, like a parent, a teacher, or a religion, but it can also come from the social consciousness of any group we identify with. There are usually written and unwritten rules that we are expected to adhere to.

The first challenge we face on the road to maturity is to overcome an uncritical reliance on outer authority. This is the authority that tells us what the rules are and how we are supposed to behave.

Overcoming our reliance on outer authority doesn't necessarily mean we no longer follow these rules, but it does mean that we no longer *blindly* follow them. It is the uncritical part that is the problem.

But if we can't just follow the rules given to us by an authority, then who or what do we follow?

Closing the Authority Gap

Transitioning out of the age of authority means we begin to think for ourselves and start to make our own choices, independent from outer authority.

When children hit puberty there is often a period of rebellion. What do they rebel against? The rules! They want independence and to start making their own rules.

It's a period of deciding which rules to keep and which to get rid of, shifting away from blindly following outer authority and learning to rely on inner authority. It begins the process of learning discrimination, often through experimentation.

During this transition we have to shift from following an outer authority to following our own authority. That inner authority means we have to find the answer by relying on our own experience, critical thinking skills and ultimately on our own heart.

When the guards in the experiment stepped into their role, there were two forces pitted against each other, an outer and an inner force. One guard was clearly reluctant to embrace his role. After the warden talked to him about the need to be tough, he later said in an interview that it wasn't until the second day that he decided to fully take on the role. He literally had to force himself to shut off his feelings towards the prisoners.

It shows the inner and outer forces at play. He initially followed his heart, but then consciously chose to override his feelings— closing his heart—to resolve the conflict between the outer and inner forces.

The guard in this case decided to stop listening to his inner authority and fell back on accepting the outer authority as his guide.

Closing the authority gap doesn't happen overnight. It's a process. We've closed the authority gap when we've developed the inner strength to forge our own path.

The Age of Self

When we leave our reliance on outer authority behind, we enter the age of the self. This stage means we have the inner strength to make our own decisions, while—in most cases—still lacking the discrimination and life experience to make good decisions.

This stage is characterized by viewing life through a selfish and often political lens. We often see ourselves as the victim of circumstances and of those with more power than us. While before we were looking for safety, now we seek the power to satisfy our desires. The downside is that most of the people who want power have not yet the experience and maturity to use it responsibly.

We have within us an unerring compass, a way to tell if the action we're about to embark on is right or not: our conscience. When it's functioning, this moral compass can steer us through the shoals of life.

This voice of our conscience can be strong or soft, and some people appear not to hear it at all. Those who can hear it don't always have the strength to follow it.

That, in a nutshell, is our inner truth, the truth that resides in our heart. We can hear it, or we can't. We have the strength to follow it, or we don't. This is the second challenge.

The guards that became enamored with their role, and the power it gave them, either couldn't hear their conscience, or if they could, they didn't have the strength to follow it. The part of them that loves power and loves to be in control asserted itself, and it didn't take long before they began to abuse their power.

For some people, power has an almost intoxicating effect. Much like alcohol or opioids have the ability to turn some of us into addicts, power, too, can act like a powerful drug.

For those who are susceptible to it, it is like any addiction, corrupting our judgment. It keeps us from finding and following the voice of our heart.

Lance Armstrong might know a little about that.

As a seven-time winner of the Tour de France he rode to the heights of fame and success and then was stripped of his titles because he did it in a way that earned him the almost universal scorn and contempt of his former fans. He doped. He lied. He attacked and destroyed people who spoke the truth, dragging them into court and accusing them of defamation. He had a lot of power, and he didn't hesitate to use it, even on his—formerly—closest friends.

It was never about being right; it was always about keeping his addiction going. Addicted to being the star, being in the limelight, even rubbing shoulders with presidents. Like any addict, he was lost and completely disconnected from his conscience.

According to David Walsh, a journalist who admits to having been obsessed with trying to expose Lance for years, he could very well have gotten away with it if he had decided to stay retired. But even staying retired was hard. Perhaps he was suffering from withdrawals after being the hero and the center of attention for so long.

His decision to get back in the game did get him more attention, but it also brought back the accusations of doping, and this time they began to stick. It became harder and harder to deny the truth, and in the end he went on national TV and admitted that his accusers had been right all along. He won every one of his Tour de France titles because he used performance enhancing drugs.

When he went on the Oprah Winfrey show, she asked him point blank how he felt about what he had done, and the picture that emerged was not of Lance being full of remorse.

Oprah: "Was it a big deal to you, did it feel wrong?"
Lance: "No, it's scary."
Oprah: "Did you feel bad about it?"
Lance: "No, even scarier."
Oprah: "Did you feel in any way that you were cheating?"
Lance: "No, the scariest."

He apparently didn't *feel* what he did was wrong, he didn't *feel* he was cheating, and he didn't *feel* bad about it. He couldn't hear his conscience.

Clearly, he was not ruled by an outer authority. He felt no guilt for not following the rules. But his inner authority had not yet uncovered what was in his heart. Instead, his desire for fame, power and money ruled the day.

There are a number of feelings and emotions that can cover up our heart, and with it, the voice of our conscience. Lust for power and money—or any other addiction—will do it, but feelings of anger, fear, shame and guilt can do it too.

When these feelings become habitual, they continue to crowd out the voice of the heart. These then become habits we need to overcome if we are to uncover our spiritual core which resides in the heart.

Self-Mastery

Transitioning out of the age of self takes effort. This effort takes the form of working on ourselves. We begin to see our own responsibility and start to recognize the need to master our own ego. This initiates the journey of self-mastery where we begin to bring strong emotions like fear and anger under control.

During this stage we develop self-reliance and self-respect, which includes the recognition that we need to stand up for ourselves when needed. When we bring our egotistical side under control, it creates room for an increased awareness of our heart and its moral compass.

The Age of Integrity

At this stage we begin to lead with the heart. We know our heart and listen to it, viewing life through a spiritual lens. With full access to our heart, we are aware of and follow our moral compass.

We are interested in freedom, making a life that is the best we can make it, for ourselves, our loved ones and for anyone else in our circle of influence. Our actions are never based on trickery, deceit or coercion, but are guided by the principles of love, truth and freedom.

This stage is characterized by responsibility. Taking responsibility for our own life, the good and the bad in it and taking responsibility for improving it. It also includes taking responsibility for how our actions affect others.

We develop a keen interest in understanding what is truth and what is not. We learn to discriminate—recognize which people have an honest take, and which people are simply promoting an agenda.

We make an honest and concerted effort to treat ourselves and others based on the golden rule, with kindness, respect and love. We respect every individual's right to life and liberty. We stand up to those who cross a boundary with us, not with anger or violence, but with firmness.

In this category we find the guards in the experiment who had to be counseled to be tougher, to become the stereotypical tough guard. But their heart wasn't in it. Instead of following the rules they were given, they followed their heart. They ended up giving the prisoners little gifts like an apple or a cigarette. They were kind.

When the heart matures it reaches a tipping point. When we begin to lead with the heart, there's a shift in priorities. The outer scorecard loses importance, while the inner scorecard gains in prominence and they switch places.

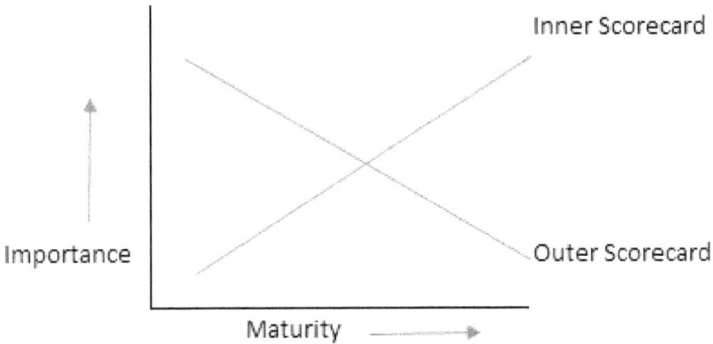

Figure 5.2

When we allow the heart to lead, things begin to change in surprising ways. The heart has its own logic and its own ways of realizing truth. The simple shift that occurs as we begin to lead with the heart instead of our head can lead to a greater sense of responsibility for our actions.

It doesn't mean that we stop using our head. But we recognize that our heart holds the key to making ethical decisions and choose to follow its lead when the situation calls for it.

That's what Nadav did when faced with a dilemma.

A Choice of the Heart on Mount Everest

On May 19, 2012, twenty-four-year-old Nadav Ben Yehuda started the final ascent to the top of Mount Everest. Years of preparation were about to pay off; summiting Everest would make him the youngest Israeli ever to make it to the top.

But as he closed in on his goal, less than 300 meters shy of reaching the summit, he saw someone lying on the path in front of him. When Nadav recognized him, he stopped. It was Aydin Irmak, a fellow climber he had met only recently, at base camp, and they had developed a friendship.

Irmak had already reached the summit but had collapsed on the way down. He was barely conscious, and without gloves, crampons or oxygen, he was simply waiting to die. Other climbers simply stepped over him, continuing their climb to the top, but Ben Yehuda made a different choice.

When he recognized his friend, he started yelling his name, to make sure he was still alive.

When he saw that his friend was still alive, he lifted him, clipped him to his harness, and then began the incredible task of carrying him all the way back to Base Camp IV, the last camp before the summit.

Every year some mountaineers don't make it. They collapse and turn into frozen corpses that litter the path to the top. Irmak would have been one of twelve casualties that year, except for one thing: Nadav didn't let that happen.

He made a choice of the heart.

Ben Yehuda told reporters, "It was very difficult to carry him because he was heavy. From time to time he regained consciousness but then turned off again. When he came to, he screamed in pain, and this made our descent even more difficult."

To make matters worse, Nadav's oxygen mask broke and along the way he lost his gloves, but nine hours later he carried Aydin into the camp. With serious frostbite, but alive, they were evacuated by helicopter to a nearby hospital in Kathmandu.

Both men survived the ordeal, to live another day and climb another mountain.

Nadav Ben Yehuda led with his heart.

A lesser man would have gone for the summit instead. He would have set a record—the youngest Israeli ever to make it to the top of Mount Everest. Quite a feather in his cap.

But he didn't. It took strength to make that choice. Both physically and morally he chose the harder path. Carrying his friend for nine hours, in a freezing, low oxygen environment.

No doubt his head had very good reasons why it would have been better to scale the summit instead. *They only knew each other for a short time. It was every man for himself, and what did he really owe his friend? In fact, Aydin was possibly already beyond help.*

But his heart had the strength to override that kind of thinking. This is what happens when the heart matures. It gains wisdom and strength, and little by little it begins to lead. In this case his heart knew he couldn't leave his friend to die. He had to try and save him, not knowing if he would succeed or not. He had to try, even though that meant giving up his chance to scale the highest mountain in the world.

Most of the time our head and our heart can work seamlessly together without a conflict. But in this situation, he had to make a choice, one or the other, the summit or his friend, his ego or his conscience, the head or the heart. If he had chosen to go for the summit, no one would have faulted him, no one would have known the price he paid for it. But it would have weighed on his heart for the rest of his life, and he wasn't willing to pay that price.

Summary

- Just like we can learn with our head, we also learn with our heart. This spiritual education leads to a more mature state of the heart.

- As the heart matures, we move through different stages. As we progress through these stages, we eventually learn to make better decisions and become more able to listen to and follow our heart.

- When the heart matures, it reaches a tipping point, where the head and the heart come into balance, with a tilt towards the heart. We begin to lead with the heart.

- With a mature heart we can see life more clearly, and we can navigate it with more wisdom, more kindness and more love.

Chapter 6

Closing the Authority Gap

Science is the organized skepticism in the reliability of expert opinion.

—Richard Feynman

Jeannette is neurodivergent. That means her brain doesn't work the same way most people's brains do.

"I love to learn, but I hated school," she recalls. "If there were things that were hands-on and tactile, like art and geometry, then I really enjoyed the process of learning. But subjects that required more linear and analytical thinking were very hard for me."

By the time she got to fifth grade she was diagnosed with Attention Deficit Hyperactivity Disorder (ADHD) and her parents found a charter school for her with lots of hands-on activities. That helped her brain to learn with more ease, and she loved her time there.

The experience that followed at her Catholic high school was a different story. "Going into this more conservative community was a hard adjustment for me," she says. "The dogma that was taught there didn't sit well with me. One religion teacher told me I had to change my viewpoint in a paper I had written, or he would fail me. I couldn't do that because that would be a lie!"

She had a small group of friends but felt inadequate because they all seemed so smart while she had to work so hard to make

Closing the Authority Gap

passing grades. "That was really hard for me. I had very low self-esteem throughout high school," she says.

After high school she didn't want to go to college. Anticipating the struggle it would be, she didn't want to make herself suffer through that. She decided to spend time in Costa Rica instead, working on a sea turtle conservation project. She loved her time there, being in the middle of nature.

After Costa Rica she came back to the States and became a nanny for a doctor and his wife. Besides giving her room and board they would pay for her to attend community college, but things didn't go as planned.

The family she stayed with had everything: a beautiful house, a great job and lots of money. But, as it turned out, they were very unhappy. They were never present with each other and ended up filing for divorce. It made her question the American dream. When she saw that what is being marketed in our culture as the "right" path was an illusion, she spiraled into a depression. When on top of that a close friend of her died, she felt totally lost.

Dealing with deep emotions was very hard for her, in part due to her neurodivergence. Without the emotional support of family and friends Jeannette's way of dealing with her emotions was to starve herself. She compares it to alcohol or drug abuse. "At some point your body is so deprived of nutrients that you don't feel anymore. Your brain is not even functioning. It helps to suppress those deeper emotions," she explains.

For two years she was in and out of treatment centers but didn't feel like they were helping her all that much. At one point a doctor told her that she would be dead by twenty-one. This awoke the rebel in her, and she decided she'd show him he was wrong.

Healing Through Food

She began to question what the doctors were telling her: an

important turning point. A dietitian told her that you can eat an apple or a bag of skittles and it doesn't make any difference, it turns into the same thing in the body. She looked at the woman and told her, "That's nonsense!⁵"

"It was a shift to learn to trust myself instead of an outside authority," she notes. "I knew that what I eat affects the way my brain works, and the way I think. This put me on the path of wanting to study psychology and learn more about health and nutrition. I felt drawn to all the research about the way our microbiome affects brain health. This is where I first learned that nutrition doesn't just affect depression, it also affects ADHD."

Through her schooling she continued to discover different types of therapeutic eating. These eventually helped her heal her gut, and then other things began to heal. Her road to recovery was far from a straight line though.

"I failed miserably at first. I tried raw veganism after listening to an inspirational speaker. I thought: This man is so vibrant, he's so bright, so articulate and energetic. I want to know what he's doing, and I want to try that."

She tried a raw vegan diet in the middle of winter in Minnesota, and it was awful. "My digestion was terrible, I was super depressed, and I was cold all the time." Then she thought she must not be doing it enough, so she soldiered on. Next, she began to develop food allergies, and she finally had to admit it wasn't working for her.

Still convinced that diet held the key to her healing, she tried the GAPS (Gut and Psychology Syndrome) diet next. It incorporates healthy fats and eggs, and it takes out foods that are inflammatory like refined sugars. This stabilized her blood sugar, and she noticed that she was able to focus much better throughout the day.

---

⁵ She may have used a more descriptive term which I leave to the reader's imagination.

"Besides changing my diet, I also incorporated adaptogens. These are herbs that help the body to restore balance, like ashwagandha, rhodiola and bacopa. Those really helped with restoring my cognitive function as well."

Still on the vegan bandwagon, she was hesitant to add meat to her diet. She had environmental concerns about eating meat, but as she learned that animals could be raised using regenerative practices, she began to eat meat. She literally felt like a part of her brain that had not been functioning suddenly turned on.

By experimenting, she discovered that her body thrived on having more protein and healthy fats. It was a real eye-opener for her that she could listen to her body and let it tell her which foods were giving her better focus throughout the day, and which foods had the opposite effect.

Everyone Is Unique

"I believe that everyone is their own unique ecosystem, and I had to become a scientist in my own life, to realize what works for me. Even though proteins, healthy fats, and blood sugar stabilization really helped me, it might be different for somebody else."

When I asked her what she is most grateful for, her answer surprised me. "My struggle with mental health. It allowed me to ask those bigger questions early on."

Jeannette sees the struggle she had with depression, ADHD and anorexia as a gift because they helped her grow.

"It gave me humility. I can't judge people based on their life experiences. Initially I had very much the idea that my way was the right way. I wanted to help my family and told them: If you just did this then you would fix your problem.

"I've come to realize that the way they process their emotions, and the way their brain works, is so much different than mine. It has given me the capacity to become a better listener and to be more present with them. To be able to ask better questions. That ultimately was more helpful for them to find their way and find what was best for them.

"I know what it's like to doubt myself, and to give my authority to someone outside myself who knows 'better'. Because of my ADHD I've had to learn what works for me. My greatest gift is to give other people in my life that same respect and let them have their own journey to discover what's right for them."

Jeannette's neurodivergence was instrumental in helping her make the transition from following outer rules and authority to learning to follow her own authority. It's more a process than an event.

It usually means experimenting, as she did with different foods, discovering what worked for her and what didn't. But even then, when she tried to follow a diet that clearly wasn't working for her, she still forced herself to continue, based on the authority of the person who recommended it.

Closing the authority gap means shifting our authority from the outside to the inside; trusting our body when the signals it's giving us don't line up with what a doctor or other authority tells us.

We may need to close the gap in different areas. Parents, doctors, scientists, newscasters, teachers, priests and politicians all end up in roles of authority. The point is not to stop listening to them, but to recognize that they're human like the rest of us. They might be wrong.

The tradeoff is that once we close the gap, we are consciously assuming responsibility. When we choose to follow the advice of a doctor or a teacher, it is our decision. When we tune into a news station that is spreading lies or hatred, it is our choice to listen to it or find another one that doesn't.

It puts all the responsibility where it belongs—on our shoulders.

Milgram's Experiment

In the 1960s Stanley Milgram did a series of experiments. He wanted to understand how it was possible that so many people in Nazi Germany went along with the atrocities perpetrated by that regime. The answer that so many individuals gave during the Nuremberg trials where Nazi war criminals were prosecuted was that they were "just following orders."

So he devised an experiment to test our response to authority. His findings surprised everyone, including himself.

The experiment which was billed as a "learning experiment", involved a subject who was instructed to give an electric shock to another person each time they made a mistake. With each mistake the shock voltage increased, going up all the way to 450V.

The idea was to find out how far the subject would go. In reality no one was receiving an actual shock, but a recording was played after each "shock" that made it look and feel to the subject like it was real.

Each time the subject would begin to resist, the experimenter as the person in charge would tell the subject to continue with an increasingly authoritative sentence, starting with "Please go on" and ending with "You have no other choice. You must go on."

The experiment went through multiple iterations. On average, 65% of participants went all the way, delivering the experiment's ultimate shock of 450V.

Let's pause for a moment to reflect on this. The individuals participating in this experiment received $4.50 for their time. Then they were asked to give a series of increasingly strong electric shocks to another person—the learner—whom they couldn't see, only hear.

Every single person in the experiment continued to give the shocks up to the 300V threshold. Only 35% stopped before getting to the 450V shock. The other 65% continued even though they heard the "learner" cry and beg them to stop. After the maximum shock was administered there were no more cries, just silence. If this were real life, they might have just killed a person, simply because someone with authority told them to do so. That's how strong our impulse to follow authority is.

The results were no anomaly. The experiment was duplicated multiple times, across cultures, countries and gender. It wasn't their culture that had predisposed Germans to be obedient in the face of authority. The results of the experiment point to a much broader application: It's a human predisposition.

We were all born with a default setting, and it tells us to follow authority. After all, we are not born equipped to survive on our own. We need to trust authority figures—parents and teachers—to teach us how to survive.

But this setting is meant to change when we grow into adulthood.

Babies have fontanelles, soft spots that allow the skull to flex when going through the birth canal. After birth, these soft spots begin to strengthen and close, and for most of us they've completely closed by the time we're eighteen months old.

Nature designed us that way. With age-appropriate weaknesses, that will strengthen once we've passed through the phase for which they were designed.

Blind trust in authority is a survival mechanism that serves us well during childhood, but like the fontanelle, it is a weakness, a gap that needs to close when we become an adult.

The results of Milgram's experiment tell us that only a third of adults actually do close the gap, at least in the area of morality and ethics.

We all know that killing another person is wrong. It's not due to a lack of knowing. But what then sets the 35% apart from the rest?

Misplaced Trust and Loyalty

Becoming a functional adult means we have to change our default "trust authority" setting. We can no longer trust people with authority unconditionally. Instead of blindly trusting and following an outer authority we need to follow our own inner authority. This is what adults do—developing sound judgment and relying on our own authority.

Jeannette made this shift when she realized that an expert who was supposed to guide and help her told her that there's no difference between eating a box of skittles and eating an apple. She knew better, because it contradicted her own experience.

It was a pivotal moment for her because it began the realization that her life was up to her. She needed to make her own decisions, and she was responsible for the result of her actions.

Once we realize that it is up to us to choose who to listen to, who we trust, who and what we follow, we take our first step into maturity.

Although the initial realization is often this aha moment that helps us make the shift from outer authority to inner authority, this is only the beginning of a lengthy process. Maturity takes time; it's something we grow into. But engaging with the following questions can help move the process along.

1. What is meaningful?
2. What is truth?
3. What is justice?

Each of these questions may elicit a wide variety of answers, depending on who you ask.

How we answer these questions has a direct impact on how we navigate our life.

What is meaningful gives us a direction. What is truth provides us with a map of how we view reality. And what is justice provides us with a moral compass.

None of these are easy questions to answer. Rather, they reflect an ever-changing understanding. The answers to these questions evolve and change as we grow and have more experience to draw on.

They are personal to each of us. What is meaningful to me may not matter to you. Truth often depends on the lens or lenses with which we view reality. If justice were cut and dried, the court system would not be so full of people suing each other.

Maturity is the result of a shift inside us. This shift happens when we realize that there are some questions that nobody can answer for us. That is, almost anybody is willing to answer them for us, but therein lies the rub. If you are going to let someone else answer these questions, you still have to decide who's answer you like the best. Who's your champion for truth? Who best exemplifies justice?

The 35% in Milgram's experiment who refused to go all the way had a level of spiritual maturity. They were able to stand up to the pressure because they had developed their ability to listen to their heart. They had a strong sense of self and knew their boundaries.

Perhaps the reason there was very little scientific follow-up to understand what made this group different is that this is a spiritual quality. Science and spirituality are on different tracks; they are two different ways to expand our understanding of reality.

Science uses observation, logic and reasoning, so it improves our intellectual understanding. Spirituality is based on an awareness of the spiritual laws and realities, and this awareness comes through the heart.

At some time before they participated in this experiment, they found their answer to *What is justice?* and chose to live by a code of ethics. When the man leading the experiment pushed them to deliver a shock beyond the danger level, they had the clarity inside to know they would be crossing a line. Beyond that, they had built the strength to be consistent with their personal code. They had closed the authority gap.

We are always subject to pressures. It can be peer pressure, pressure by a salesman, a doctor, or pressure from your spouse or your kids. No matter how much pressure we receive, we will need to live with the consequences of what we do. Maturity means we've learned to listen to the opinions of others and then make our own decision. We recognize that no matter what other people say, no matter how much pressure they give us, the responsibility for our choices, and the results they bring, is ours.

Following Our Moral Compass

What prompted Milgram to conduct his experiment were the atrocities committed by the Nazis during the second world war. Even though the war brought out the worst in some people, there were also those with a more developed sense of justice, like Jan Zwartendijk and Chiune Sugihara.

Zwartendijk was heading up the operations for Philips—a Dutch manufacturer of electronics—in Kaunas. In May 1940, as he was leaving for the day, the phone rang. It was De Decker, the ambassador for Estonia, Latvia and Lithuania, asking him to take on the role of acting Consul for the Kingdom of the Netherlands in Lithuania.

They had only met once, and Jan was surprised to say the least. The previous consul had resigned, and Jan agreed to take his place for the time being, not really knowing what to expect.

This was happening against the backdrop of a quickly escalating war: Germany and Russia (then USSR) had invaded Poland. France and the UK had declared war on Germany, and Germany had invaded the Netherlands. It was a time of great upheaval and uncertainty.

Many Polish Jews had fled to Lithuania after Germany invaded their homeland, but that was at best only a temporary solution. Many realized that the German war machine would eventually come to Lithuania as well, so they tried to leave, and to do that they needed a visa. The problem was that no country was willing to take in the Jews and give them the life-saving stamp in their passport.

This was the situation facing Zwartendijk when he agreed to be the acting consul. As he had to navigate this rapidly shifting landscape his moral compass was what guided him.

Peppy Levin, one of the Jewish refugees, had worked with De Decker to come up with a creative solution. In the end De Decker had added a note in her passport saying that no visa was needed for some of the Dutch colonies, including Curaçao—omitting the fact that the decision for entry would be up to the Governor of the colony.

It wasn't really a visa, and Jan didn't think it would hold up, but when she asked him to do the same for her husband and her relatives, he realized it could potentially save their lives, so he was willing to do it.

This was the beginning of a steady stream of Jewish refugees who came to him for the same entry in their passports. With Curaçao as the final destination, they could go to the Japanese consulate and get a transit visa.

The Japanese Consul, Chiune Sugihara, faced a sea of faces, all coming to ask him for a transit visa to Japan. Understanding the plight of the refugees, he sent a telegram to the Japanese Foreign Minister, asking him if he could issue the visas. The answer was clear: No visas were to be issued unless the traveler had a firm end visa outside Japan and guaranteed departure date from Japan.

This created a conflict for Sugihara. Thousands of refugees showed up on his doorstep, and it was in his power to help them. His heart told him to help them, but his superior had given him a direct order not to. He talked it over with his wife, knowing that issuing the visas could mean he would lose his job. They decided he would go ahead and issue the visas anyway.

For weeks he spent every moment from early in the morning to late in the evening brushing the Japanese characters in the Jewish passports, giving them a way out of their current predicament. He wrote and he wrote. Every time he completed another visa he would return the passport to the owner, look them in the eye, and wish them good luck.

After Lithuania was invaded by the Russians, Sugihara was ordered to close the Japanese consulate. He asked for, and received, an extension, all the while issuing visas. But on August 28, 1940, time ran out and he had to close the consulate for good.

He would leave for Berlin a week later, and as he stayed in the Metropolis hotel, people found him, and he continued to issue more visas. On the day of his departure he was still writing visas, even as he boarded the train.

With both the Dutch pseudo-visa and the Japanese transit-visa in their passports, the refugees could get a Russian exit-visa and buy a train ticket that would take them through Russia, all the way to Vladivostok, and from there they could board a ship that took them to Kobe in Japan. None of them continued on to Curaçao.

Even though Japan and Germany had become allies in the war, Japan never adopted the same antisemitic practices that drove the Germans to exterminate millions of Jews. In Japan the Jews were relatively safe, and the large majority of them were able to survive the war there.

Sugihara and Zwartendijk knew they were taking a risk, unsure what price they might have to pay for their actions later. But they chose to act on what their heart told them to do, issuing over two thousand visas.

Sugihara was reassigned to different European posts during the war, and he and his family ended up in a Russian prisoner camp where they were kept until 1947 when they were finally allowed to go back to Japan.

This is when he had to pay the price for issuing the visas: He was asked to resign from the civil service and had to find menial jobs to provide for his family. They went from living a life of status and wealth to living in poverty.

For Zwartendijk there appeared to be no negative consequences. He continued to work for Philips after the war, and he never spoke about issuing the visas.

When decades later a story came out in *B'nai B'rith Messenger of Los Angeles*, a Jewish paper, that talked about the "Angel of Curaçao," nobody really remembered his name. The article did prompt Dutch government officials in charge of foreign affairs to inquire what his role had been, which resulted in an interview he did that was printed in a Dutch newspaper, the *Leeuwarder Courant*.

Soon afterwards, he received an invite from the Dutch foreign ministry to come to The Hague. The conversation he had there was not what he expected. He was literally reprimanded for what he had done. According to the ministry he should never have done what he did in Lithuania. He had broken the rules, so he would never be eligible for a decoration.

It's not like Zwartendijk cared about being decorated, but to be reprimanded for what he did felt humiliating to him. It's true that few organizations reward people for breaking the rules. But being reprimanded for trying to save thousands of lives would leave anyone with a bad taste in their mouth. It shows the tone-deaf culture of the foreign ministry at that time, led by Joseph Luns, who himself during the war had been part of the NSB, a Dutch political party that collaborated with the Nazis.

Both Zwartendijk and Sugihara were reprimanded for their actions by their governments. They could have done the expedient thing and followed the rules. But that's not what good people do when there's a conflict between the rules and their moral compass.

They were good, decent people, who acted on what their heart told them was the right thing to do. They knew they might have to pay a price for it, but not acting when it was in their power to help these people conflicted with their conscience.

Ethics. Conscience. The golden rule. A moral compass. Goodness. Respect.

Different words looking at the same thing from different angles. They are an indication of a mature heart. A heart that insists on treating others with goodwill, decency, and respect. A set of priorities and guidelines that allow us to discriminate between what's right, good and decent, and what's not.

When we allow the heart to take precedence over outer rules and authority it's a sign of maturity. It doesn't mean we have to defy authority at every turn. It means that when we're asked or ordered to do something, we always run it through an internal check first.

This is what the 35% in Milgram's experiment did. They took the instructions they were given and weighed them first and then decided to follow their inner authority.

The other 65% went along with whatever was asked of them. Perhaps they thought of saying no but didn't want to rock the boat. Or perhaps they didn't even consider it at all.

Still, they must have known something wasn't right about what they were told to do.

Like Chiune Sugihara knew what he was told to do was not right. But often there's a gap between knowing and choosing to follow that knowing. It takes inner strength to follow where the heart leads.

Self-confidence and inner strength are essential to closing the authority gap. You have to feel confident enough in your own judgment of a situation, and care enough to follow it. Even if large numbers of people disagree with you, even if it puts you in an uncomfortable spot.

Summary

- The authority gap is the default setting of unconditional trust with which we approach authority early in life.

- To become a functional adult, we need to close the gap and change this setting from unconditional to conditional trust. This means we need to shift from relying on outer authority to relying on our own inner authority.

- Inner authority is the result of discrimination. We discriminate between right and wrong, truth and illusion, those people who are honest and operate on a set of moral principles and those who do not.

- Relying on inner authority requires that we listen to our heart and build an inner framework. The framework guides us when we need to decide what's true, what's important and what is the right thing to do.

- Three questions that can help build this framework:
  – What is meaningful?
  – What is truth?
  – What is justice?
  The realization that nobody else can answer these questions for us is a necessary step on the road to maturity.

- Self-confidence, inner strength and listening to our heart are essential to closing the authority gap. We have to feel confident enough in our own judgment of a situation, and care enough to follow it, even if other people disagree. This takes courage.

Chapter 7

The Moral Compass

The battle line between good and evil runs through the heart of every man.

—Alexandr Solzhenitsyn

The Secret of Power

There's a parable about an old king with three sons (there are always three sons in these stories). Each of them wants to take their father's place when the old king dies. The king needs to make a decision about which of his sons should take his place when he dies, so he creates a test.

He calls them into his throne room and tells them that whoever inherits the throne will have a lot of power. He tells them there's a secret about power he wants them to discover. Whoever discovers the secret will be the one to inherit the throne. He tells them to come back in a week and each of them has to tell him what the secret of power is that they discovered. After this he will make his choice and decide which son will become his heir to the throne.

The first son decides to go to the leader of the army, and he asks him about the secret of power. The general looks at him thoughtfully and then speaks.

"Power is a force of nature. In battle you ride that force like a stallion. If you ride it well, you will be swift and decisive and gain victory over your opponent. The secret of power is to be fearless in the face of danger."

The second son decides to go to the richest man in the kingdom, and he asks him about power. The man thinks about it for a moment. Then he speaks.

"Power is in the way people perceive you. When you are rich, other people will envy you and fear you, because you can do whatever you want. You have absolute freedom. What is better than that? You can build monuments in your own honor. Eat the best food every day, and you will have no difficulty finding a beautiful woman to spend your life with. The secret of power is that it gives you absolute freedom."

The third son decides to go to a wise man who lives in the forest. (Wise men always live away from the rest of us, usually on a mountain, but this one prefers the forest.) When he finds him, the wise man is just making dinner, but he looks calm and undisturbed by his royal visitor. "How can I help you?" he asks.

The prince tells him he is in search of the secret of power, so he may inherit the throne from his father, the king. The wise man walks inside and comes back with two cups. Then he pours water into the cups. The first cup immediately begins to drip, and the water slowly drains, forming a puddle on the table. But the second cup holds the water.

The wise man points to the first cup and says: "That cup is no good." Then he points to the second cup. "That one is good. There is your secret of power." The prince's confused look prompts him to go on. "Power is like water. The holder of power is like a cup. If the cup has integrity, it holds the water, and it can be used for a proper purpose. But if the cup has a crack, the water leaks out and ends up in the wrong place. A person who holds power needs to have integrity, to know how to use the power and when to use it to make things better. Without integrity, even when used with good intentions, it will make things worse."

When the sons return, their father calls them back into the throne room and asks the first son what he learned.

The first son kneels and tells his father that the secret he learned about power was that power is a force of nature that needs to be ridden like a stallion. When he inherits the throne, he will lead the army and extend the kingdom by conquering neighboring lands.

The king bends over and kisses him lightly on the left cheek, knowing this son isn't ready to wear the crown.

The second son kneels and tells his father that the secret he learned is that power lies in controlling the perception of the people in the kingdom. He would use the money in the treasury to build large statues of the king and a new palace to impress on them his greatness.

The king bends over and kisses him lightly on the right cheek, knowing this son isn't ready to wear the crown either.

The third son kneels and tells his father he isn't sure he learned anything of much value. But the secret he found is that power is like water and that whoever is holding that water needs to be a cup that doesn't leak. All he could promise was that he would use the power as little as possible. The army, only to protect the border. The money, mainly to fix things that are broken, and to further leave the people in the kingdom be, to do as they see fit.

The king bends over with tears in his eyes. He kisses him on both cheeks, knowing that he has at least one son who's ready to wear the crown.

What is Power?

Power is the ability to create an effect. More power means the ability to create a greater effect.

Although power is in essence a neutral force, it is also the source of much abuse. It is like electricity. In nature electricity wreaks havoc by creating fires through lightning strikes. Uncontrolled, it is a destructive force. By gaining a better understanding of it, we learned that it is a form of energy, and we discovered there are many ways to use it constructively.

Like energy, power is neither good nor bad, but it becomes good or bad, depending on how we use it. Like electricity, it needs to be controlled, or it will become destructive.

When people come into a position of power who are lacking either the inclination or discrimination to know how to use it for good, the power flowing through them becomes as destructive as a lightning storm.

Owning The Post

Philip Graham was an alcoholic, suffering from depression. On August 3, 1963, he took a shotgun and ended his own life.

His wife Katharine had a decision to make. Her father had bought *The Washington Post* when it was in bankruptcy and had turned it around. Then he turned it over to Phil, who ran it for a couple of decades until he committed suicide.

After Phil's suicide several potential buyers offered to take *The Post* off her hands. Should she sell it?

She loved the paper, and she cared about the people. To her, *The Post* was a family heirloom, and there was simply no way she would sell it.

She decided to learn how to run it herself instead.

When she took ownership of *The Post* and stepped into her new role, she had none of the experience or qualifications needed to run the company. But she did have one important qualification: She loved the paper and cared about the people she employed.

It wasn't easy. She was a woman in a man's world, and a woman with no experience in business whatsoever. In the 1960s businesses run by women were far and few between, and attitudes towards women in the workforce were only just beginning to shift.

Closing the authority gap in those days was a lot harder for women than for men. As she notes in her autobiography *Personal History*, she had a lot of insecurity to overcome.

By deciding to run *The Post* she got a front-row seat observing all the ways in which attitudes about women in the workplace were at work. She was facing these attitudes from the almost entirely male workforce, but many times she realized these attitudes were ingrained in her as well, and it took time to discard them.

In time she came to the realization that it was simply up to her. She had to do the job in whatever way she could do it, without trying to be someone else, especially Phil. She had to find her own way.

The Pentagon Papers

Less than six years after Katharine stepped into her new role at *The Post*, Richard Nixon also moved into a new role. His election as the next President of the United States set the stage for a face-off between the press and the power of the state, wielded by a president who was not weighed down by an abundance of scruples.

The first tangle between *The Post* and the White House arrived when *The Post* came into possession of the Pentagon Papers. The Nixon administration went to court to try and stop first *The New York Times* and then *The Post* from publishing them.

It was a big decision. She was well aware that publishing the Pentagon Papers could destroy *The Post*. "But," as one of her editors said, "there's more than one way to destroy a paper."

It took courage to decide to move forward, and she did. The lawsuit filed by the administration was escalated through the courts until it ended up on the docket of the Supreme Court. The Court ruled that the government had not met the burden of showing justification for restraining further publication of the Pentagon Papers. This cleared the way for *The Washington Post* and *The New York Times* to continue publishing the Pentagon Papers.

This loss in court notwithstanding, the government continued to harass *The Post*.

It is important to understand how governments operate. The government is made up of people who gravitate towards power. They intend to use that power, and news outlets need to have a strong spine to stand up to it. It's a sad fact that the executive branch quite often tries to control and intimidate the news and social media.

The Pentagon Papers were not really the threat to national security that the government claimed, but they did provide an overview of the actions and decisions that led to the United States becoming more and more involved in the Vietnam war. These were decisions that had preceded the Nixon White House, and yet the administration fought all the way to the Supreme Court to keep them secret.

Why did the Nixon administration try so hard to keep this information from being published? From time to time a government comes into power that feels it ought to control what people know and believe.

There's a natural tension between a healthy press corps and the government. The government controls the power of the state. The press needs to report honestly and fairly on the use and abuse of that power, and that frequently causes some tension.

It certainly took a healthy and tenacious press corps to pursue the next story that would put *The Post* once again in the crosshairs of the President.

Watergate

In June of 1972 five men were caught breaking into the headquarters of the Democratic National Committee, located in the Watergate office building in Washington D.C. Two reporters from *The Post*—Woodward and Bernstein—were put on the story that little by little turned into one of the most influential stories in the political history of the country.

The tension between *The Post* and the Nixon administration continued to grow as the story unfolded, and more members of the administration were shown to be involved. Woodward and Bernstein continued their coverage under a barrage of attacks, persistent accusations and a concerted campaign of intimidation. The closer their investigation took them to the White House, the stronger the White House attacks on them became.

Katharine notes how the constant attacks were effective and taking their toll. It made her wonder how long they could survive this kind of strain.

This was essentially a fight that could not end well for one of the parties. It was the White House against *The Washington Post*. Nixon was furious and Katharine heard through multiple sources that Nixon vowed to get her once he was reelected.

The reporting by *The Post* on Watergate had little effect on the elections; Nixon won reelection by a landslide, carrying forty-nine out of the fifty states.

Repercussions followed soon after. The Post owned two television stations in Florida whose licenses were up for renewal and their renewals were challenged. The Jacksonville station had three challenges while the station in Miami had one. There were over thirty stations in the state of Florida up for renewal and these two were the only ones challenged. It was hard not to see this as the administration following through on its threats.

To make matters worse, leads on the Watergate scandal dried up, creating the appearance that the whole thing had been a personal vendetta by Katharine against the President. Nixon certainly seemed to see it that way. It was perhaps hard for him to understand that the reporters at *The Post* weren't pursuing this story because Katharine told them to. Their loyalty, more than to the owner of the paper, was to the truth. It went to the heart of their purpose as reporters, to turn up the truth and make it available to the public.

And although their reporting had led to several convictions, there was no guarantee that they would be able to get to the bottom of it.

The public's perception about Watergate began to shift when one of the defendants in the case, James McCord, agreed to tell everything he knew. In exchange for a lenient sentence, he was willing to talk. He claimed that perjury was committed at the Watergate trial, and that defendants had been pressured to plead guilty and keep quiet. He said that higher-ups were indeed involved, and that several members of his family had expressed fear for his life if he disclosed knowledge of the facts in this matter.

It was the first domino in a slow chain-reaction that brought out ever more facts that continued to lead to the President. Another key domino was the revelation that there was a voice-activated recording system in the White House. It was good luck for *The Post* that the tapes had been preserved and had not been "accidentally" destroyed.

In a final crescendo Nixon tried to keep the last domino—the White House tapes—from falling by what became known as the "Saturday Night Massacre." Special Prosecutor Archibald Cox demanded that the tapes from the White House be turned over as evidence. Nixon resisted and eventually instructed Attorney General Richardson to fire Cox. Richardson refused and immediately resigned. Richardson's deputy, Bill Ruckelshaus, also refused to fire Cox, and he resigned as well. The next man in line at the Department of Justice was Robert Bork and he did fire Cox on the President's orders.

This led to several impeachment resolutions that were introduced in the House of Representatives.

In the end, the tapes were released, and they provided the evidence that President Nixon had been aware of the break-in and had been actively involved in the cover-up. Rather than facing impeachment, Nixon chose to resign.

That brought the extended fight between the President and the press to an end.

It was an extraordinary time where the Republic functioned as intended. First the press, and then Congress, held the President and his administration to account for abusing the power of the state.

Both Katharine and Nixon had moved into a position of power. They had closed the authority gap and had shifted to following their own authority. When we follow our own authority, we can either be motivated by love or power.

When motivated by love, there is respect for all the right things—for the truth, for the property of others and the freedom to make their own decisions. This is how it was at *The Post*. Katharine cared about the people, and she cared about the paper being truthful and fair.

While reporting on the Watergate story, the editors made sure certain rules were followed. If information came from an unnamed source it had to be supported by at least one other, independent source. Even though much of the information came from confidential sources, they double-checked the story through multiple sources before it went to print. The same care was taken with stories reported by other papers and media outlets. They didn't run it unless they could verify and confirm it through their own reporters. It was important to them that what they reported was factual and true.

With these guardrails in place Woodward and Bernstein had total freedom to run with the story.

The Nixon White House operated under very different rules that were based on a political worldview. In this view might makes right, and what you do isn't wrong unless you get caught. People motivated by power often try to control and bend other people to their will. In general, when people are drawn to a position of power it is because they want to use it. In their eyes force is the best way to solve a problem.

Love and power underlie many of the attitudes and beliefs we hold, and they form the lens through which we view the world.

There is a saying that we see things not as they are, but as we are. This seemed to apply in Nixon's case. He believed Katharine was out to get him—she wasn't. He thought she ran *The Post* the same way he ran the White House, demanding that people work on projects based on her personal whims—she didn't.

Their conflict was as old as the ages. It was the clash between two different levels of maturity.

When the Nixon tapes from the White House were finally released to the public, the world was aghast at the callous and profanity-laced comments that came out of his mouth. Directing his anger about government whistleblowers towards Jews, he said, "Go after all these Jews. Just find one that is a Jew, will you?" In a conversation with Henry Kissinger, he called India's female prime minister, Indira Gandhi, a bitch, mentioning how "We really slobbered over the old witch."

An overall lack of respect for Jews, women, and a total disrespect for the law. All par for the course at the adolescent stage, dominated by a self-centered viewpoint, and a political lens.

At this level there are two dominant and immature beliefs that stand in the way of following our moral compass:

1. *The end justifies the means.*
   It is the flawed reasoning that is most frequently used to justify the use of force or deception to reach a specific goal and get something done.
2. *Us against them.*
   Rather than seeing people as individuals, we see people in terms of groups or tribes. This tribal thinking causes us to treat people based on our opinions about the group they are a part of, rather than their personal actions and character.

These beliefs are often fueled by strong emotions like fear and anger. Fear and anger cover up our moral compass.

Politics encourages us to view life through a political lens with the kind of tribal thinking that is as common today as it was during Nixon's presidency.

The whole Watergate affair was the result of a break-in that was fueled by the belief that the end justifies the means.

Katharine Graham, at the mature end of the spectrum, followed her moral compass. She recognized that the means are as important as the end, and in most cases more important.

Instead of using a political lens, she chose to see life through a lens of integrity. Motivated by a deep respect for the truth she had a simple vision for *The Post*: to realize its potential and make it the best paper it could be.

Summary

- The moral compass is the basic choice between love and power.

- Everyone has a moral compass, and it resides in the heart.

- A mature person has learned to listen to his heart and developed the strength to follow it.

- There are two lies and two emotions that have been used by authorities throughout history to manipulate the masses, justify immoral behavior and bypass our moral compass.

- The two emotions are anger and fear. Fear closes the heart. When fear or anger is strong, we can no longer make good decisions. We can't hear the voice of our conscience, and that means we're primed to accept the two lies.

- The two lies:
  1. The end justifies the means.
  If the goal we are pursuing is good, we can do so without regard for individuals and their rights. This can be used to justify almost any action.
  2. Tribe trumps individuality.
  Tribal thinking means we treat an individual based on the group they are a part of rather than on their individual actions or character. It comes into play when one group intends to use force on another group and tries to take away their rights.

Chapter 8

Life, Our Personal Obstacle Course

Yesterday I was clever, so I wanted to change the world. Today I am wise, so I am changing myself.

—Rumi

"I was tremendously afraid of the world. That's all I knew. I didn't have a word for it and didn't know I wasn't supposed to be like that."

Daniel was an extremely fearful child.

Although the separation anxiety he experienced when going to preschool is not uncommon, most children adjust. In his case it was a sign of a bigger and more persistent problem. He was very anxious about physical safety. His mind conjured up robbers and murderers, even though he lived in an affluent and safe community in Marin county, California.

In elementary school he managed his anxiety with the support of his teachers and a psychotherapist. But it continued to have a big impact on him: racing thoughts, stomach pains, and even feeling nauseous in places like restaurants and movie theaters.

In fifth grade his father enrolled him in Taekwondo, hoping to boost his confidence.

"The martial arts did help me with my anxiety because it made me feel physically safer. Physical safety was a big issue for me."

Through middle and high school, he kept training in martial arts, trying out different styles. After Taekwondo he moved on to kickboxing and later mixed martial arts until he joined the Novato boxing gym. Despite all his martial arts training he still had trouble standing up for himself when bullies in school gave him a hard time. He had the physical skills to defend himself, but he hadn't yet fought the battle within.

Anxiety impacted his sleep and that in turn affected his grades. In high school it made him do worse in math and science because those were the subjects he was most worried about.

A big shift happened for him soon after he graduated high school.

"One day while walking I felt a deep sense of peace and happiness, even though nothing in my outer life had changed. This helped me realize that peace can be an inward thing; it doesn't have to come from my outer circumstances.

"I began to see that what I thought was reality was really how I perceived reality and how I thought about it."

This was perhaps the first time he realized that he was not his thoughts. He had an extreme pessimist in his head, giving a running commentary on the terrible things that could happen to him at any moment. This negative self-talk had kept him in a state of anxiety for most of his childhood—until he realized he could take charge.

"I began to study spirituality and psychotherapy on my own. I realized that the thoughts I entertain and my responses to them were really the cause of my lifelong anxiety. If I can change my thoughts I can change my feelings, and if I do that, I can change my reality.

"I started to become very aware of the thoughts that were causing anxiety in my life. I began to ask myself: In two or three years from now, will the thing I'm anxious about really make a difference?"

It was one of the techniques he used to manage his thoughts. This process of reeducating and conditioning his mind into a more relaxed state took years, but it worked.

"From eighteen onward I began to see myself very differently, and I began to be treated differently by others. I went from having poor and mediocre grades to being a high-achieving student. I started dating more, which I had had a hard time doing because of my anxiety. The way I saw myself and the way others saw me changed tremendously."

By taking charge of his thought processes, he was able to turn his life around. It had taken a fair amount of self-discipline, as building new habits does.

And then he had a crazy thought. *What if I challenged Amir Khan to a boxing match?*

With that thought several things fell into place. Challenging his favorite boxer to a match would surely bring up lots of anxiety. Then he could use the techniques he had already been using successfully to overcome his anxiety and write a book about it.

With a bachelor's degree in psychology and a desire to help others overcome their anxiety, the idea appealed to him, and he decided to go for it.

He contacted Khan and proposed his plan but was declined. Undeterred, he tried one of Khan's opponents, Phil Lo Greco, a professional boxer holding several titles, but who had lost to Khan through a knockout. "I posted on his YouTube channel, his Instagram, any place I could connect with him."

Soon, he received an email from Lo Greco suggesting they should talk. In the phone conversation that followed Daniel explained his idea, talked about his anxiety and the book he was planning to write. Lo Greco got on board with the plan, and they agreed to set up a match in Toronto.

At that time Daniel had a few years of boxing experience at the local boxing club. A far cry from the professional boxer he would face in the ring. To prepare for the bout, he began to train in earnest. Physically he had to get in the best possible shape, and as expected, his anxiety flared up.

"I didn't sleep very well that whole five-month period while I was preparing for the boxing match with Lo Greco."

Daniel managed his anxiety by controlling his perspective. When showing up to a training session exhausted because of lack of sleep, his self-talk would start up. *I'm exhausted, and I'll show up to the fight exhausted.* Then he'd remind himself that there were lots of nights before the match and he would have plenty of opportunities to sleep and be well rested.

He monitored his self-talk and replaced all negative thoughts with better ones. He also used mindfulness, meditation and breathing to calm his nervous system. And most of all, he kept his eye on the prize: an opportunity to write a book and have a dual career in both psychotherapy and writing.

When the big day arrived and he stepped into the ring, he soon realized how far out of his depth he was. "I was very limited in skill compared to Lo Greco. It was very clear to me he could really hurt me, and I could walk into a very big punch.

"During the second round Lo Greco landed a big punch that took me by surprise. I was immediately flooded with my biggest fear, that I would sustain a brain injury."

Fortunately, that didn't happen, and they decided to end the match with a round where there were no hits to the head, only body shots. "I was very ambitious in that round, I wasn't as fearful, and I did much, much better in that round."

The fight ended up having a big impact on his life.

"After the fight I was treated like an actual athlete, almost like a sports hero. Everyone wanted to know about my book and about the fight.

"As people's perceptions of me changed, so did my perception of myself. I saw myself as much more capable. The fight raised the bar really high for what would cause anxiety in me. Compared to before the fight, it would take much, much more to make me anxious."

It was a rather drastic way to change his self-image, but it worked.

Actions speak louder than words, even the words we tell ourselves. Using the as-if principle, he acted as if he were fearless and confident. By doing this he created a new reality with diminished fears and greater confidence.

Finding Our Spiritual Core

Michaelangelo once said that when he created the sculpture of David he could already see him inside the block of marble. All he had to do was carve away everything that wasn't David.

We are in a similar position as Michaelangelo, except we are our own masterpiece. Everyone has a core of goodness and love, but in most of us it's covered up.

It is up to us to find the spiritual core that's locked inside, and that usually means we have to remove everything that isn't part of that core.

This process is different for every one of us; it is a personal, custom-made obstacle course. All obstacles are of our own making, but only some are of our own choosing. Daniel didn't choose his anxiety, but he had to deal with it anyway.

Common ways in which we cover up our heart are shame, blame, fear and guilt. And there's the lust for power. The extent to which we are able to clean up these habits, attitudes and beliefs marks the progress we've made towards a more mature heart.

The idea of self-mastery is not new, but few people went about it with as much zest as Ben Franklin did a couple centuries ago.

As an enterprising young man Ben was making a go of it as a printer in Philadelphia. He recognized how important good habits were for success, and he set out to master thirteen habits that he saw as necessary or desirable.

He listed them in his autobiography as follows:

1. Temperance.
Eat not to dullness; drink not to elevation.
2. Silence.
Speak not but what may benefit others or yourself; avoid trifling conversation.
3. Order.
Let all your things have their places; let each part of your business have its time.
4. Resolution.
Resolve to perform what you ought; perform without fail what you resolve.
5. Frugality.
Make no expense but to do good to others or yourself; i.e., waste nothing.
6. Industry.
Lose no time; be always employ'd in something useful; cut off all unnecessary actions.
7. Sincerity.
Use no hurtful deceit; think innocently and justly; and, if you speak, speak accordingly.
8. Justice.
Wrong none by doing injuries, or omitting the benefits that are your duty.
9. Moderation.
Avoid extremes; forbear resenting injuries so much as you think they deserve.
10. Cleanliness.
Tolerate no uncleanliness in body, clothes or habitation.

11. Tranquility.
Be not disturbed at trifles, or at accidents common or
unavoidable.
12. Chastity.
Rarely use venery but for health or offspring, never to dullness,
weakness, or the injury of your own or another's peace or
reputation.
13. Humility.
Imitate Jesus and Socrates.

He soon discovered that trying to change all his habits at once
didn't work, so he created a system. For a full week he would focus
on a single habit. For each day of the week, he tracked how often
he fell back into his old habit. The goal was to have a full week
without any marks. For the second week he would move on to the
second virtue and focus on it for a week. He deliberately set out to
change his habits and build the habits that would lead to success.

It took him thirteen weeks to practice each of the virtues. Then
he would start from the beginning, so that in a year's time he
would go through each of the virtues four times.

He created a table to track his progress, by drawing the
following grid (figure 8.1) in a notebook.

How did it all work out for Ben? To say that he became a success
is an understatement. He built a flourishing business as a printer.
He became the postmaster general. He experimented with
lightning and electricity and invented the lightning rod. He
became a statesman and an ambassador, helping to birth a new
nation.

	Sun	Mon	Tue	Wed	Thu	Fri	Sat
T.	*	**			***	*	
S.							
O.							
R.							
F.							
I.							
S.							
J.							
M.							
C.							
T.							
C.							
H.							

Figure 8.1

Could you benefit from improving your habits?

If you are willing to put some effort into building new habits, you might consider using Ben Franklin's system for self-mastery.

Self-Mastery Exercise

Create a list of habits that you know or suspect are working against you. For each habit identify the new habit you want to replace it with until you have a list of positive habits you would like to develop. You

105

can add a short description of the new habit, similar to what Ben Franklin did.

Here's an example of some common negative habits and the positive habits or virtues to replace them.

* Fear ⟹ Courage, positive self-talk
* Shame ⟹ Self-acceptance, self-love
* Blame / Anger ⟹ Forgiveness, tolerance
* Impatience ⟹ Patience
* Guilt ⟹ Self-forgiveness
* Laziness ⟹ Self-discipline

Ben Franklin's thirteenth virtue (humility) was added at the recommendation of one of his friends who mentioned how Ben tended to be rather proud. We all have blind spots, so if you have a spouse or a close friend, someone you trust, show them the list and ask them if there's any habit you missed.

Once you've completed your list, you've planned your work. Then it's time to work your plan and put it in a grid like Ben did, so you can start tracking how well you're doing.

Habits can be hard to change. Our mind and emotions tend to form grooves. Like water running down from the mountain they can form deep riverbeds that take time to change. It took Daniel years of facing his fear and anxiety before he was able to change those patterns. Be patient with yourself if you are unable to change your habits quickly but stick with it.

Our personal obstacle course often includes things like fear, anxiety and a negative self-image. Once we have learned not to love and respect ourselves, or worse, that we're not worthy of love and respect, it can take a supreme effort to overcome these false beliefs. Feelings about safety and identity run deep. It can take all our strength to overcome such negative thoughts and feelings. But it can be done.

Healing a Negative Self-Image

Gina's mom grew up in Japan, where keeping up appearances is deeply ingrained in daily life. Gina grew up in America, but her mom raised her and her siblings in Japanese fashion with a strong focus on their looks, and a constant concern of how things looked to the outside world. "If you didn't meet her standards, you were considered damaged goods," she told me.

Gina did not measure up. She repeatedly received the message that she was no good, not worthy, there was something very wrong with her. Not pretty enough, not the right personality. Over time, it stuck, and she began to believe it too.

A sensitive child to begin with, she became even more introverted and retreated further into herself. In school she was so quiet that she was given separate counseling sessions to bring her out of her shell. It didn't quite work. The programming she received at home was not so easily reversed. She had learned her lesson all too well: She was unworthy of love and consideration.

When she entered the workforce, she wanted to only work with computers.

"I used to work the weekend shift, and I would be a computer operator and a tape operator. I didn't want to talk to people, didn't want to see them, and didn't want them to see me. I just wanted to work in a data center and be around machines. That was easy and safe."

But there was something that called to her. The freedom of the open sky. At twenty-four, she decided to act on a lifelong dream, and she started taking flying lessons.

"That was a huge change. It woke me up from just existing," she said. "There were some miracles that began to open me up: the joy of flying, going to Toastmasters and meeting my future husband."

It was a turning point in her life. She realized that flying meant she would need to talk to the control tower, and that got her motivated to get over her shyness. Toastmasters—an organization that allows people to practice public speaking—was where she began to take charge of her fears and learned to speak with confidence.

Still, all wasn't well.

There was still this feeling inside, this little girl that felt unworthy of love. For years she thought that if she achieved certain goals, she would start to feel better about herself. If she was thinner, if she got her bachelor's degree, and then her master's degree. If she got a promotion for a more important job with a better title, then she would feel better about herself. She achieved those goals, but these outer scorecard successes never quite managed to fix her inner scorecard problem.

"Even though I had certain status, certain titles, I still felt there was something wrong with me. I didn't fit in. I would retreat to my own darker place. I knew I was still a bad person, and I was just creating this illusion for others," she recounts.

She went through some dark times and even contemplated taking her own life. She needed help but wasn't sure where to turn when she reached out to her neighbor, Ginger.

"She's a dear soul. I think of her as an angel. She wasn't pushy, but it was her gentleness, compassion and sense of humor that attracted me to her," she remembers.

Ginger invited her to a Bible study group. She did start to attend, but she initially found it hard to relate to.

"Just because I say I'm a Christian doesn't mean that everything is automatically okay. You have to put forth an effort to have that relationship, just like any other relationship," she said.

She stuck with it, but it took several years before she found herself saying: "Ha, I finally get it!"

That's when things shifted for her. Through prayer, and really making a connection, not just going through the motions.

This is when God became real for her. She could hear God talking to her and feel the love and closeness in her heart. It brought an unexpected healing: She started feeling better about herself and was finally able to let go of her deep-seated feelings of unworthiness.

She still considers herself an introvert. But once she gets to know people, she enjoys their company. Today she rates herself as an 8.5 on the Inner Scorecard, a far cry from the time she was thinking about suicide.

Gina faced a giant obstacle. Her mother gave her the message that she was not good enough, not valuable, and therefore not worthy of love. Children have no defenses against such messages, and she accepted them unconditionally. It became her truth.

This set the stage for a rough childhood and potentially a loveless life. Even when she worked hard to earn the respect of others. Even when she had a husband who loved her. She still felt inside like it was all a charade, because she still held the belief that she was not worthy of love and respect.

The reason it changed was that she had a spiritual experience.

It is one thing to be a Christian—to believe in God and read the Bible—it is another to be spiritual and develop a relationship with God. When this relationship became real for her, she began to experience the divine love that helped to change and heal the belief that she was not worthy of love.

We are all worthy of love, no matter how unworthy we may feel. But knowing this with our head is not the same as knowing it in our heart. The healing happened when she was able to accept this in her heart.

Such is the power of divine love.

Gina shared another observation with me in response to the following story that I shared with her.

As a teenager I was riding my bicycle over a small bridge when three kids on bicycles came from the other side. As we crossed on the narrow bridge one of them hocked a loogie and it hit me right in the face. He was laughing with his friends, so excited and proud of what he had just done. They stopped to see what I'd do. Would the fun continue? If I had challenged him to fight it would have been three against one. I chose not to. But the frustrated feeling of humiliation and the injustice of it all did fuel my desire to learn to protect myself.

A week later I joined the local karate club. I worked hard and over the course of several years, I earned a black belt.

The reason I had shared the story was to highlight how I used to wear an invisible "kick me" sign. Which is a way of saying I didn't feel good about myself, and other kids picked on me because they picked up on that.

Choosing to learn karate changed how I felt about myself. I no longer was on the receiving end of any loogies once I decided that I had value, and I was worth fighting for.

Gina mentioned that the difference between her and my experience was that I knew I could change. She never knew she had that option. She felt that her lot in life was to suffer. Even worse, she simply felt that any abuse was expected behavior towards her and that she deserved that kind of treatment.

She carried this fixed mindset with her, that she was unlovable, and that there was nothing she could do to change it.

A belief like that is devastating, and it can stop any potential for change and growth in its tracks.

Our personal obstacle course means we need to clean up these attitudes and beliefs that keep us from being our best self.

The Power of Belief

A positive belief in ourselves and our ability to change can be like a rocket that fuels our success in the world while negative beliefs are the chains that tie us to unhappiness and failure. While a positive belief won't make us successful by itself, it is part of the fuel we need to be successful.

While barely out of elementary school, Warren Buffett declared he would be a millionaire by the time he was thirty-five. He reached that goal when he was thirty; by thirty-five he was well on his way to the $10M mark.

We will never outperform our beliefs about our own limitation.

Any belief in our own limits may keep us from success. We do have real limitations, but often the belief in our limitations is the real limitation. We are capable of so much more than we think. The belief most conducive to success is that we have *unlimited potential*. We also have real limitations. Where the two of them meet is the edge of growth.

Take George Dantzig, a first-year student at the University of California in Berkeley. He walked into class late one day, and he assumed the two math problems on the blackboard were homework, so he copied them down.

When he started working on them, he noticed the problems seemed harder than usual and it took him a long time to complete them. When he was finally ready to turn in the homework he apologized to his teacher, Mr. Neyman, for taking so long to complete it. Was it still okay to turn in the homework late? "Just throw it on my desk," was the answer. He did so, with some misgivings, because the desk was littered with a heap of papers. He half expected his homework to get lost in there forever.

Six weeks later, on a Sunday morning, he was awakened by someone banging on his front door. It was Neyman. Full of excitement, he said: "I've just written an introduction to one of your papers. Read it so I can send it out right away for publication."

Not understanding what any of this was about, George was confused. What paper? He eventually discovered that the two math problems on the blackboard had not been homework at all. They were two famous unsolved problems in statistics. He solved them because he thought they were homework. He believed he should be able to solve them, and so he did.

The power of belief can unshackle our mind. It can also work as a drag that holds us back.

The psychologist Carol Dweck delved into the influence of what she calls a fixed mindset versus a growth mindset.

She discovered that the stories we tell ourselves when we perform poorly on a test or some other task have a big impact on our ability to learn and improve. The stories reflect our underlying belief.

I'm just not smart enough. I will never be any good at this. These are stories that reflect a fixed mindset. In contrast we can tell ourselves, *I can get better at this, if I put my mind to it. If I study hard, I will get better.*

People with a growth mindset tend to explain their poor performance by lack of studying or preparation while those with a fixed mindset believe their performance was because they're not smart enough.

When we carry around a fixed mindset, it can be almost impossible to create positive change. In other words, whether we believe we can change, or whether we believe we can't, we're right.

Our beliefs have enormous power. They shape our behavior, our perception, and they shape our life.

And no belief is more destructive than the belief that we are not worthy of love and respect.

Self-respect is the belief and the knowingness that we have value and are worthy of being treated with kindness and respect.

Summary

- We don't all come into the world equal, nor are these inequalities random. Life is a personal, custom-made obstacle course. All obstacles are of our own making, but only some are of our own choosing.

- Self-respect is an essential aspect of maturity. It means being assertive, able and willing to stand up for ourselves. It also means having a healthy level of self-esteem, realizing our value and worthiness to be loved and protected.

- Negative beliefs—like shame, blame, fear and guilt—often stand between us and self-respect.

- A fixed mindset acts like a drag on success. A growth mindset can unlock the potential within.

- A growth mindset recognizes that negative habits and beliefs are obstacles that can be overcome. How well we manage the obstacles—those placed in our path and those we engage by choice—determines our success.

- We can shape our habits and beliefs for success.

The Integrity Code

Part Three

The Three Pillars of Integrity

It's not intention that drives the outcome of actions and laws, but integrity. The way to be a force for good is to act with integrity.

Chapter 9

The Integrity Model:
A Blueprint for Success

Integrity is your destiny. It is the light that guides your way.
—Plato

"Mr. President, I don't see it." The President looked puzzled. "Pardon me?" he asked. "I just don't believe these photos present credible evidence of weapons of mass destruction," said O'Neill, "and I advise against using this evidence to justify an invasion."

The grainy satellite photos that were presented as proof that Saddam Hussein had stockpiled biological, chemical, and nuclear weapons, did not convince Paul. And they certainly didn't meet the level of proof he believed was needed to start a war.

After his comment the room fell silent. He had just broken the cardinal rule in President Bush's administration. Bush demanded absolute loyalty from his staff, and Paul had challenged him.

It wasn't the first time Paul's propensity to speak the truth put him in the crosshairs of the commander-in-chief. Paul couldn't stand the kind of loyalty that was expected of him.

To him that was a false kind of loyalty. He believed in loyalty, but not in blind loyalty, regardless of what a person might say or do. Real loyalty in his mind was based on telling someone your best understanding of the truth, and not necessarily what they want to hear.

What became increasingly clear was that Paul and the President weren't on the same page about the priorities for the country. This, eventually, led to Paul being asked to resign.

When then President-elect Bush asked Paul to become a member of his cabinet, he agreed. The reason was that as Secretary of the Treasury, he hoped to take advantage of the several years of budget surpluses. He could do something meaningful: fix Social Security and pay off the national debt. He could see how putting the country on a sound financial footing for many years to come was within reach.

As we now know, history took a different turn. Instead of fixing Social Security and paying off the national debt we got a tax cut and a war, and federal deficits as far as the eye could see.

O'Neill did make some sweeping changes within the Treasury, while running it for almost two years. He brought the lost workday rate down by about 50%.

One of the things Paul had strong feelings about was that people should never be injured at work. The lost workday rate was a key measurement for worker safety, and he made it a cornerstone of his management philosophy.

Before his time at the Treasury, he was CEO at Alcoa, the largest maker of aluminum in the world. After he was selected for the job, he thought about what he wanted to be remembered for once he left. Worker safety was at the top of his list. This was the most meaningful thing he could come up with, and being the CEO, he could implement changes that were on the top of his "most meaningful things to-do list".

It certainly didn't endear him to investors who were initially scared off by all his talk about worker safety. They had likely never encountered a CEO before who led primarily with his heart. Paul was driven more by his caring about people than by budgets and profits.

In his first few days at the company, he visited a factory because he wanted to get a feel for the environment and the people he was now responsible for as CEO. While eating in the lunch hall, someone asked him to give a speech. He did, and he talked about worker safety. He told them that he wouldn't budget for safety. To him every safety issue was so important that it would need to be taken care of right away, without thinking about the budget.

He did something else that was unusual. He gave them his personal phone number and told every worker to call him if there was a known safety issue that wasn't taken care of right away.

Two weeks later he got his first phone call. A big machine in one of the factories had broken down and hadn't gotten fixed for several days. The result was that people had to move a 900 lb. slab of aluminum manually from one place to another. That could easily cause a back injury or worse, it could fall on somebody's foot.

O'Neill made a couple of phone calls, and the machine was fixed right away. In the following month he received one or two more calls, but then it stopped. He called it the internal tom tom system. Word got around that the new CEO meant what he said about worker safety.

This wasn't enough though. Paul also made sure there was a team that looked at every injury that occurred. The team's job was to analyze it and recommend a solution. He wanted this posted on Alcoa's website. That way every one of the more than one hundred worldwide locations could see it and avoid having the same problem.

He understood that most of us care more about people than we do about numbers. That's why he wanted every injury to be listed with the name of the injured person—something his lawyers strongly recommended against, but he did it anyway. He didn't want these real people with real injuries to turn into just another statistic.

What did all this lead to? It created a culture of caring, a prerequisite for creating a culture of excellence. As O'Neill mentioned, "I believe that excellence at its best is habitual." At the root of this habit is the question *How can we make things better?*

Paul had a clear vision for the organization and how to make it better. Not surprisingly, it was based on the people. He believed that every person in a great organization should be able to answer these three questions with a wholehearted "yes":

1. Am I treated with dignity and respect by everyone I encounter without regard to race, status, rank, gender, educational attainment or any other distinguishing feature?
2. Am I given the resources, tools, training, and encouragement to make a contribution to the organization that adds meaning to my life?
3. Am I recognized for that contribution by someone whose opinion matters to me?

This is an organization that runs on love and love asks the question *How can I make things better?* It is how excellence comes about, by people who put their heart into what they do.

Paul certainly cared about excellence, and he was able to inspire and motivate the people he worked with to do the same. His focus was on excellence, realizing that that's how you create value.

He believed it was better to focus on the root cause than the result. He said that "In a truly great organization finance is not an objective, it's a consequence. And it's great if it's the consequence of being more excellent than anyone else that does what you do. In my experience, the finances follow excellence."

That's not to say that he didn't care how the finance department was run.

During a chat with the Chief Financial Officer (CFO) Paul asked him how much time it took to close the books at the end of the quarter. Eleven days. Then he asked him if everything was set up right and all tasks would be lined up without delays and all systems were properly integrated, how long it would take. A week later the CFO got back to him. Three days.

"Okay. That's your new goal, to close the books in three days," Paul said.

It took over a year to get there, but they did. He had a way of making people reach for excellence.

The Integrity Model

Integrity Model	LOVE	TRUTH	FREEDOM
Personal	Provides meaning, purpose and joy. Respecting ourselves and others.	Honesty, fairness and excellence	Choice and agency. Self-mastery, self-determination, self-reliance.
Universal	Serving others. Treating people with respect and goodwill. Do no harm.	Laws of nature, spiritual laws. How things are and how thing work.	Power. Limited by our role and our environment.
Commitment to Integrity	Becoming a force for good.	Discover and honor truth.	Honor and respect freedom in yourself and others.

Figure 9.1

Paul's leadership was based on principles. He said, "Leadership is not about writings on the wall; it's about acting in a noticeable way on the principles you established so that people begin to believe that they are real."

Good leaders are first good followers, and they follow sound principles.

The integrity model revolves around three principles or rules. Each principle is needed and is balanced by the other principles.

When these principles come together in a balanced way the result is integrity.

To achieve a goal with integrity we need to honor these three principles. When we fail to honor even one of them, we lose integrity.

Integrity matters because it is how we can improve our lives and the lives of others, without cutting corners and harming someone else in the process.

Perceived through the heart these are the values and qualities that make success meaningful. Perceived through the head these are principles and rules we follow to achieve meaningful success.

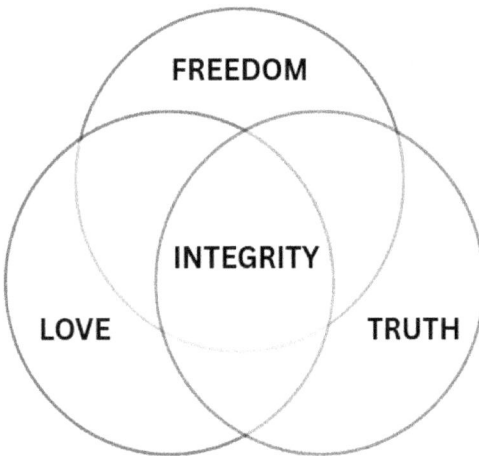

Figure 9.2

Love, Truth and Freedom.

The first principle is love. Love is our why—the primary driver of what's meaningful to each of us. Love means caring, and Paul cared deeply about worker safety, something he recognized as being part of the dignity and respect each individual deserves.

But love is more than a feeling; it's about perception and action. Paul didn't just care about the people in his organization, he took action. He did his absolute best to prevent them from being injured at work. Love sets things in motion by taking action.

Love is the secret sauce that propels us out of mediocrity into excellence. Paul's blueprint for a great organization is one that is fueled by love and thereby delivers excellence.

The second principle is freedom. Freedom is a composite of internal and external factors. We all have freedom of choice and a certain amount of agency, but our ability to act can be hemmed in by external factors, as Paul was when he was Secretary of the Treasury. He didn't have the freedom to implement his full vision there because of the mismatch between what was meaningful to him and the priorities of the President. At Alcoa he had more freedom to implement his own vision.

Internal factors can be excuses, beliefs we have accepted that limit our freedom to act. When Paul worked with people, he took away their excuses. By eliminating the budget for safety, money was no longer an excuse not to deal with safety issues. Freedom is all about overcoming our perceived limitations. There are real limitations, no doubt, but many times we limit our actions—and our success—based on perceived rather than real limitations.

Paul recognized the need to empower people. We expand our freedom by building skills. He made sure people in his organization received the resources, training, and tools to be able to build skills and do their best work.

Freedom is choice. It allows us to choose what we want to do with our time and our life.

The third principle is truth. Truth is how we discover if we're on the right track. It's the actual result we achieve. To be effective we need to measure what we are trying to change. Paul used the number of injuries and lost workday rate as his measure.

We also need to understand how things work. Wishing that things will change won't make it so. He created a clear goal—zero injuries—and a system that focused on continuous improvement.

On a personal level we honor truth by being truthful. When Dick Cheney called Paul to tell him the President wanted him to resign his position as Secretary of the Treasury, he was told to say it was "because he wanted to return to private life."

Paul refused to do that. He told Cheney he wasn't willing to bend the truth just because the President asked him to. He had no problem with letting people know the President wanted to make a change and that he had been asked to leave.

We honor truth both by being truthful, and by creating solutions built on measurements and the right understanding of how things work.

Integrity and Success

Paul was an unusual leader because his primary focus was not on the outer but on the inner scorecard. Most CEOs are hyper focused on financial results, expansion, stock price, costs and budgets. Paul's focus was on what was most meaningful to him: worker safety.

When he was asked about his success at Alcoa, he said he wouldn't know if he had been successful until years later. His personal measure of success was if the number of injuries and the lost workday rate would continue to fall after he left the company.

His goal was to leave the company stronger and more viable than when he arrived. To him this meant a durable change in the company's culture. Would people continue to care enough to pursue zero injuries after he left?

During his tenure the lost workday rate dropped from 1.86 to 0.36 and the total recordable rate of injuries dropped from 9.05 to 3.13. After his departure in 1999 both rates continued to drop. By

2014 the lost workday rate was down to 0.09 and the total recordable rate had dropped to 1.15, making Alcoa one of the safest companies in the world.

At the same time the results on his outer scorecard were nothing short of spectacular. In the twelve years he was at the helm, net income for the company rose from $200M to $1.5B, leading to an 800% increase in the company's value.

That is the result of integrity at its best.

Paul believed that values create value, and the results at Alcoa seemed to underscore that belief. By honoring the values of love, truth and freedom, the company achieved broad-based improvements in safety, efficiency and profitability, while avoiding harm.

It is the blueprint for success.

While Paul kept lowering the risk of being injured on the job for every worker in his organization, he also improved the bottom line for investors. Everyone was better off as a result of his leadership and commitment to integrity.

Opposing Forces

While the three pillars of integrity outline the path to meaningful success, they are not always easy to achieve. Both inner and outer forces provide opposition.

Individually we have little control over the outer forces. But it is within our power to strengthen the three pillars. To do so means we must adopt love, truth and freedom as values we intend to make part of our character.

To strengthen love we may need to overcome feelings of shame, blame, fear and guilt.

Truth requires that we overcome the false beliefs (illusion) that distort our perception of reality. These are either the result of deliberate manipulation (lies, censorship and propaganda) or due to regular ignorance and confusion.

To strengthen freedom, we may need to deal with personal issues that are part of self-discipline, like laziness and addiction.

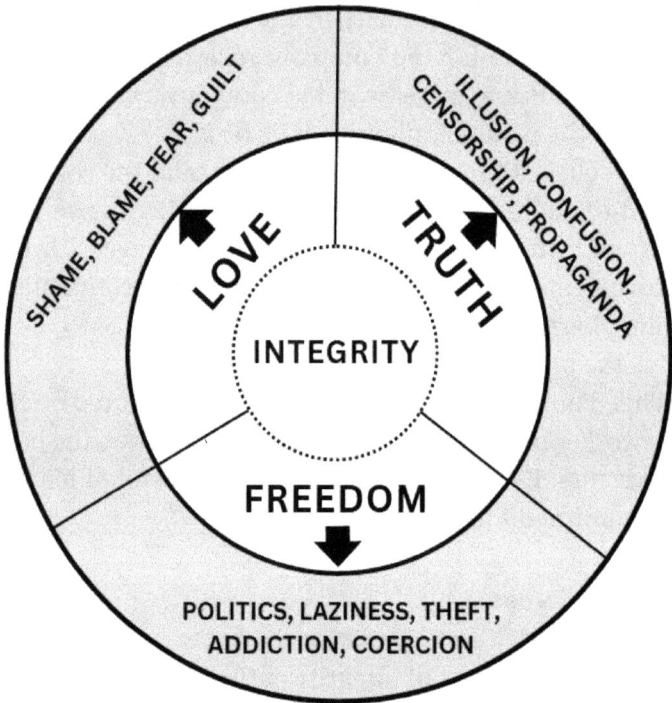

Figure 9.3

On the other hand, outer forces can and do encroach on us. There appears to be an ebb and flow to it. When national and global stressors peak, so do censorship, propaganda, fear and coercion.

The Integrity Model:
A Blueprint for Success

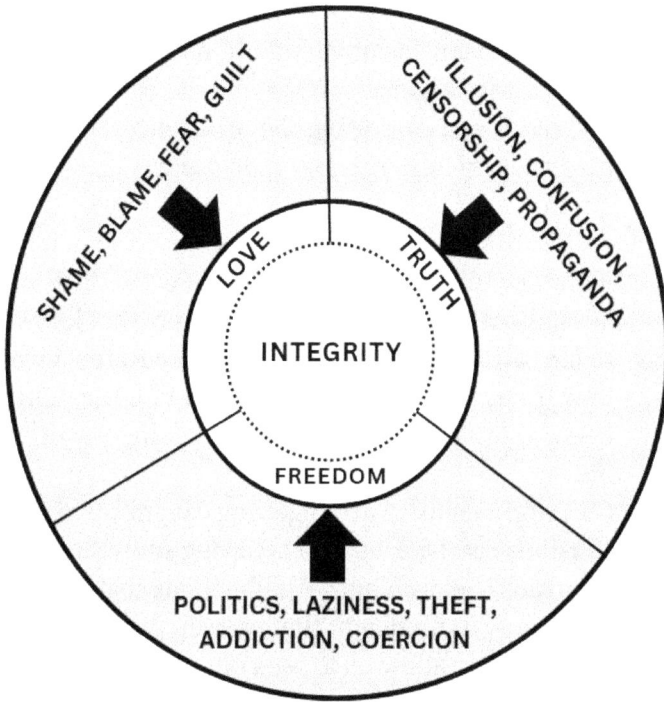

Figure 9.4

The Integrity test

There is a simple test to find out if any person, group, organization or rule has integrity.

If we look at integrity as a three-legged stool, it's clear that as soon as we remove one of its legs the whole stool falls over. Love, truth and freedom are the legs of the stool.

The integrity test checks to see if each of the three principles are present. Each principle can have both a positive and negative expression. Negative expressions are things we avoid doing, while positive expressions are things we do.

1. Love.
   (+) Love means positive intention. It asks: How can I make things better?
   (-) Love means following the prime directive of the medical profession: *First do no harm.*
2. Truth.
   (+) Truth means recognizing and working in harmony with how things work. That means we understand the laws of nature and know how to apply that knowledge to our situation. It also means we accurately measure how things are, and what the effect of our action has been. Truth tells us if what we are doing is working or not.
   (-) Truth means to avoid getting caught up in illusion. Illusions can trick us into believing something that is not true. The problem with illusion is that we can know only in hindsight that we were tricked. Curiosity and humility allow us to seek out, and stay open to, new information. Recognizing that we are all subject to the forces of illusion gives us a path towards seeing through the illusion.
   Truth also means not to deceive or engage in trickery or deception of any kind.
3. Freedom.
   (+) Freedom means we have the agency, liberty and authority to pursue our goals. Agency is the necessary skills. Liberty is the amount of freedom we have based on the rules we are subject to. Authority is the power we have based on the role or position we have.

(-) Freedom means: do not coerce. We do not encroach on the freedom of others[6].

When problems are caused by people, it is generally because someone has violated the rules of integrity.

Social Security is a system that almost every U.S. citizen pays into or has paid into in the past. There is a common belief that it is a pension system for every person who works and will one day retire.

But that's not how it works.

A pension system invests what we pay into it so that through careful money management the money multiplies and then provides guaranteed payments once we reach retirement.

Social Security is a different animal. It is one generation of workers paying for the retirement of the previous generation. The Achilles heel of this system is that it is vulnerable to demographic changes. Today we have fewer children and people live longer than they used to. The result is that Social Security will become insolvent sometime in the next decade or so. These demographic trends have been known and understood for decades, but politicians, being who they are, have not made it a priority to fix the problem.

Paul O'Neill knew there was a brief window of opportunity. For a few years the country was running surpluses instead of the deficits that had been common for decades. He had the intention to put the country on a sound financial footing by paying off the national debt and fixing Social Security (love). He understood how the system worked, what its problem was, and he had a plan for

---

[6] Children are the exception, because freedom comes with responsibility. Until children can shoulder their own responsibility, they don't enjoy the same freedom as adults.

transforming it (truth). But in the end, he didn't have the authority to execute his plan (freedom).

As Secretary of the Treasury, Paul had a freedom problem. He had good intentions and a good understanding of how to fix the problem but lacked the authority to implement his plan.

In her book *Streams in the Desert: 366 daily Devotional Readings,* L.B. Cowman relates a story about the struggle of an emperor moth.

She had cared for the cocoon of an emperor moth for nearly a year. When the moth finally began to stir, she witnessed its efforts to get out of its cocoon. All morning the moth tried to get out, but it didn't seem to be able to escape. It kept getting stuck in the narrow opening of the cocoon that was shaped like a bottle. She watched the struggle for hours and began to think something might be wrong with the cocoon. The confining fibers were probably drier and less elastic than if the cocoon had been left in its native habitat. To help the moth, she used scissors to cut off the neck of the "bottle", widening the opening.

The moth immediately crawled out of its cocoon with great ease. But instead of seeing the magnificent wings unfold themselves, she saw a creature with a large misshapen body and little shriveled wings.

She observed that her misguided effort to help the moth became its downfall. The creature could only crawl during its short existence and never was able to fly.

She later discovered that the narrow neck of the cocoon is there by design. It forces the moth to push through this narrow opening, thereby forcing the fluids from the body into its wings.

While setting the moth free, Mrs. Cowman had a truth problem. She had good intentions but lacked the knowledge and understanding of how the struggle of the birthing process was necessary for the moth's wings to develop.

The Law of Unintended Consequences

Al Capone turned twenty-one on January 17, 1920. Incidentally this was also the date that the Volstead Act went into effect— starting the era of Prohibition.

Al had been a member of the South Brooklyn Rippers and the Forty Thieves Juniors for years. These bands of delinquent children roamed New York while committing petty crimes and vandalism. But this new amendment to the constitution opened up wonderful new possibilities for the young and ambitious criminal.

The next decade turned out to be a golden age for Capone. By supplying speakeasies in Chicago and running his crime syndicate, his net worth had swelled to an estimated $100 million by 1927.

Al Capone and many of his brothers in crime took full advantage of the Eighteenth Amendment, a fourteen-year experiment in a government mandated drying out of the country better known as Prohibition.

This amendment holds the unique distinction that it is the only amendment that was repealed in its entirety. While some amendments are procedural in nature, most were added to the constitution to affirm specific rights of U.S. citizens. This amendment did something entirely different. Instead of limiting the government's power and making sure the people's freedoms are respected and preserved, it took away the freedom to produce, transport or sell "intoxicating liquor".

To understand how this amendment came to be, we need to go back to what was generally known as the Temperance Movement which started in the early 1800s. It was started by women who had a legitimate beef with the way alcohol brought out the worst in their husbands and neighbors. And not having the right to vote, they took to the streets and started to use anything from prayer to destroying saloons to try and effect change. Over time men got on board as well and they got organized in a group called the Anti Saloon League, the ASL.

The ASL was not a political party, but it gained a lot of political clout. In fact, so much so, that they had the power to get senators and congressmen elected or unseated. With their single focus on getting rid of alcohol, and their increasing power and ability to intimidate members of congress, the natural result was that more and more elected officials began to support Prohibition. It was a matter of expedience, because many of them were privately enjoying their wine and beer and were not planning on giving that up[7].

So it was mainly due to the work and machinations of the ASL that the Eighteenth Amendment was passed by Congress.

There was a widely held expectation that the law would save the government money by reducing the tax burden for prisons and poor houses, improve social problems, reduce crime and corruption, and improve health and hygiene. All these problems were thought to be caused by alcohol. The belief was that when you take away the alcohol, you've solved a whole bunch of problems all at once. The passing of the Eighteenth Amendment was the beginning of a new era where virtue would reign. Or at least, this was the expectation.

But it was not to be. Instead of virtue, the law fueled the rise of Al Capone and his ilk, financing organized crime and widespread political and police corruption. The law was a disaster. It didn't just fail, it failed spectacularly. Saloons were closed, but speakeasies—their underground, illegal counterparts—were opened to take their place almost as fast. Speakeasies had to be

---

[7] The law was written in such a way that they were allowed to enjoy alcohol from their private stash.

supplied, and they couldn't be supplied legally. So the money that flowed into these speakeasies fueled the rise of organized crime.

Homicides and violent crime went up. The government not only lost revenue from what used to be legal sales of alcoholic beverages; it now had to spend money on enforcing a law which was almost universally flouted and disrespected. The amount of alcohol consumed only fell for a year or two, after which it started to rise again. By the end of the 1920s, with the law still in full effect, alcohol consumption easily exceeded the levels prior to Prohibition.

Before the Eighteenth Amendment was passed, former President Taft saw exactly what was coming. He realized that the manufacture of alcohol, liquor and beer would simply change hands. Since law abiding citizens could no longer do it, criminals would take over.

What did he see that most people at that time did not?

For most people the law is not perceived as a guide to believe what's right and wrong. It's the same reason most of us do not consider it wrong to drive over the speed limit. Our personal moral code is not affected by the laws Congress decides to pass.

Breaking the law, for most of us, does not result in feeling we did something wrong. Only violating our personal moral code will have that effect. You can't legislate a change in people's minds and hearts. It explains why so many people did not change their drinking habits and happily made their own alcoholic brews and attended speakeasies.

When personal and social norms are at odds with the law, defiance of the law is the result.

It's perhaps one of the most extreme examples of the Law of Unintended Consequences. When we create a law with the right intention but do it in a way that fails the integrity test, the result is that the law causes more problems than it solves. Stated more concisely: *The effect of a law is not based on its intention but on its integrity.* If a law does not have integrity the effects of that law on society will be negative.

In this case the intentions were good, but you can't run roughshod over people's rights to achieve your goal, no matter how noble that goal is. In other words, the end does not justify the means. A law that indiscriminately limits freedom, like the Eighteenth Amendment, is not based on integrity.

The ASL and Congress put a law into effect that tried to take alcohol out of the area of self-control, by putting it under state-control. It didn't work. The results were so disastrous that the Twenty-first Amendment was easily passed to repeal it fourteen years later.

With that in mind, let's take a look at how the law either followed or violated the three pillars of integrity.

Love
Although the law was passed with good intentions, love also means to do no harm. Anyone making a living as a beer brewer, winemaker, or saloon owner, was forced to go out of business. They were harmed by the law, as were all the people who enjoyed alcohol in moderation.

Truth
The ASL had a strong but misguided belief that alcohol was responsible for most if not all of people's immoral behavior. There's no doubt alcohol can contribute to it by weakening our inhibitions and self-control when drinking to excess. But it is not the primary culprit. As Ben Franklin's example points out, self-control can be acquired, but it takes effort and self-discipline on our part. As the primary driver, self-control determines if we drink alcohol at all, and if we cross over the line into abuse and addiction.

Freedom
While most laws do limit our freedom in some way, the idea behind our framework of laws is that they are there to protect us

and keep us safe from harm. They outlaw behavior that causes others to be harmed. While this law didn't outlaw drinking, it outlawed the production and sale of intoxicating liquor, neither of which is inherently harmful to others. It limits freedom too broadly and in the wrong way by not making a distinction between the responsible and irresponsible use of alcohol. A law that targets drunk driving is specific, it applies to the irresponsible use of alcohol only. The Eighteenth Amendment targeted all Americans, taking away their freedom to use alcohol in a responsible way as well.

Strengthening Integrity

To strengthen integrity, it has to become a core value. This requires making a commitment to the three pillars of love, truth and freedom and developing the self-discipline to make them part of your character.

You might try the imaginative exercise below to initiate the process.

Three Ancient Warriors Exercise

In your imagination, see three ancient warriors, decked out in chain-mail armor, a helmet and each carrying a large sword. Invite these medieval warriors into your world and ask for their protection. They will form a triangle around you, facing out, they are positioned to protect you.

If you are committed to strengthening the three pillars inside yourself and being a force for good, they will be your steadfast companions and protectors.

Sworn to serve and protect, they represent the three pillars of integrity: love, truth and freedom.

If during the day someone tries to catch you in their web of illusion through lies or propaganda, tries to force you into doing something you would choose not to do, or tries to provoke you into reacting out of anger or fear, these warriors will serve as the silent protectors of your state of being.

Instead of falling for a lie you may see through it, or you may have a feeling that you should look into it a little deeper. If you have a problem with addiction, you may find a new strength inside yourself, helping you take a step towards greater freedom. When fear or anger tries to take control, you may realize you have the ability to override them.

If you make the commitment and put in the effort to strengthen these areas inside yourself, these ancient warriors will come to your aid. Know that they will help you maintain your integrity in a world that, at times, will be hostile to those who choose to be a force for good.

Summary

- Principles are the bedrock of integrity. The Integrity Model shows how the three principles of love, truth and freedom balance and strengthen each other, resulting in integrity.

- The effect of an action or law is not based on its intention, but on its integrity.

- When people, groups and systems operate with integrity the result is that things improve. Life gets better. When they break the rules of integrity it leads to a movement in the opposite direction, causing things to deteriorate.

- To strengthen integrity, we need to strengthen each of the three pillars inside us. This takes self-discipline.

- The integrity test is a simple way to assess if the effect of an action or law will be positive or negative. To pass the test all three principles must be adhered to.

- Love means: do no harm. Truth means: do not deceive. Freedom means: do not coerce.

Chapter 10

Love, the Heart of Success

There comes a time when nothing is meaningful, except surrendering to love.

—Rumi

Tom never went to college. He didn't even finish high school. But when I asked him to rate himself on the inner scorecard, he gave me a very confident ten.

He has a gentleness about him. A good sense of humor, and a quiet confidence. His eyes twinkle with good humor, peeking out from a face that is framed with a short beard and hair that has gone completely white, now that he's well into his retirement.

Tom loves his life, and he attributes this to a fundamental insight that is captured in the maxim: *If it is to be, it is up to me.*

"Once I learned to take total responsibility for the course of my life," he told me, "it became a solid ten. While you may not necessarily be able to control what you have to confront and deal with, you can always control your reaction to it. The biggest regret I have is not learning this much sooner than I did."

Although responsibility is key, he also recognizes the good fortune that has come his way. Serendipity gave him a few precious gifts that played a significant role in shaping his life.

When he was in the Air Force a fellow airman opened a drawer and pulled out a book. He said, "You might enjoy this," and threw it at Tom. The book—Ayn Rand's *Atlas Shrugged*—captivated him. It exposed him to Rand's philosophy of objectivism, which became the cornerstone of his philosophy about life.

Serendipity struck again many years later when he worked for IBM and saw this stunningly beautiful woman at work. She had an air about her as she strode confidently through the halls, in her high heels and tailored suit.

After his first marriage had ended in divorce, Tom had vowed never to marry again. But Jane, with her long blond locks, slowly but surely changed his mind. Their relationship started out purely on a professional basis, but over the years they got to know each other and fell in love.

Jane and her family were part of a particularly strict branch of Christianity, and her father held some strong views about religion and marriage. When she wanted to divorce her first husband her father had told her in no uncertain terms that she couldn't do that. It would be against God's will.

She decided to divorce her husband anyway, because she was just too unhappy. By going against her father's wishes she became the black sheep, and her whole family—with the exception of her brother—ostracized her.

When she told them she was getting married again, this time to a man who was in fact an atheist, it did not go over well. Tom and Jane celebrated their wedding with family and friends, but Jane's parents chose to show their displeasure by not showing up.

Then life created an opportunity.

Jane was offered a big promotion which required them to move to the East Coast. Tom had no interest in moving to the East Coast, but he wanted to support her, so they moved. And as serendipity would have it, they ended up living less than ten miles away from Jane's parents.

Tom had an intuition about it. A feeling that maybe he could do something about the way things were in Jane's family. It saddened him that the relationship between Jane and her parents had remained distant and cool for so many years. They had hardly even seen their five-year-old granddaughter.

"This family, from everything I could tell, used to be a wonderful community. They did things together, incredible memories from when they were growing up," he said.

He decided to see if he could help mend this fracture in the family. He realized it was risky. There was a chance he would end up making things worse. But he had the confidence to call them up, introduce himself, and ask them if he could come over and talk.

He told them, "I hate that this family has become what it has become, because Jane's told me so many wonderful things about her growing up and her family. And I want to see if we can get together and see what we can do about changing this."

They seemed to be receptive to his proposal and set up a time for Tom to come over. At the appointed time he went over to their home, where Joe and his wife invited him into the kitchen to have coffee. While they were sipping on their steaming cups, Joe gave him an intense look, then he put down his pipe, leaned across the table, and started talking.

"Thomas, isn't it a bit arrogant to believe that you're the greatest thing in the universe? That there's nothing more powerful or greater than yourself and that this amazing universe has not been created by an intelligence that is greater or higher than you and me? Isn't that a bit arrogant?"

Tom was flabbergasted and it hit him pretty hard. He didn't know what he had expected, but certainly not an attack like that. Joe picked up his pipe and with a smug look on his face started blowing more smoke into the air. It took Tom a while to process what had just happened. His goal had been to repair the relationship as best he could, and he had prepared himself not to lose sight of that.

Then an answer came to him, and he said, "Joe, we all have the same questions. I wonder where this place came from, I wonder where I came from. How did I get here? How did this place get here? It seems to me, Joe, that we all have these questions. It's just natural, it's part of our humanity. We're curious and we want to understand why.

"And along comes someone like you, and you say to me, Tom I know where we came from, I know where you came from, where I came from, and where this place came from. And I know what I'm supposed to be doing here, and I know what I'm not supposed to be doing here. And by the way, I know the same thing about you.

"Joe, it seems to me you should question your arrogance, and whom in this case is being more so."

This was followed by a long, uncomfortable silence. Joe was the patriarch, and he was not used to anyone questioning his authority like that. Tom's mother-in-law, perhaps concerned that this could lead to some serious fireworks, left the kitchen.

To break the tension, Tom started telling Joe about himself. He was hoping to show Joe that they had far more in common than they realized. And that this one thing they didn't have in common in his mind was not worth ruining what they did share.

They ended up talking for over an hour before Tom left, and they discovered they did have a great deal in common. This conversation was the beginning of mending the rift in the family. What had been a cold shoulder for years, turned into what Tom calls "a fabulous thirty-year relationship with Jane's dad and family."

Tom had the courage to walk into the lion's den, not knowing what to expect. But he knew that he had to try. Life had delivered them on his in-laws' doorstep, but it was still up to him to knock on the door and see if it would open.

He could have chosen not to. But he cared enough to take the risk. That is love, a measure of how much we care. Love always tries to find a way. A way to see past our perceived differences. A way to make things better. A way to not let differences in opinion get in the way of making a meaningful connection.

This was the case in the Supreme Court too.

A Match Made in Heaven?

Justices Antonin Scalia and Ruth Bader Ginsburg couldn't be farther apart. Scalia was a conservative judge, appointed to the bench by Ronald Reagan in 1986. Ginsburg, a strong advocate for gender and civil rights, was appointed seven years later by Bill Clinton.

They frequently argued opposite sides of a case, Ginsburg seeing the progressive side, Scalia ever the conservative. But these ideological opponents liked each other. The fact that they didn't see eye-to-eye on a political level didn't mean they couldn't appreciate one another.

Scalia had great wit, and she laughed at his jokes. They could be arguing each other from different angles at one moment and have fun together the next. Why let something as silly as politics get in the way of enjoying each other's company?

They practiced what is perhaps the American ideal: diversity and respect. They embody the notion that even though you may disagree with someone's viewpoint, you can still like and respect them as a person.

Their friendship blossomed. They would go to the opera together, and even vacation together. Friendships form because we make a heart-to-heart connection with another person.

Scalia said of Ginsburg, "What's not to like, except her views on the law?"

Despite little digs like that, they got along fine and respected each other as legal scholars. Ginsburg knew that a dissenting opinion from Scalia forced her to be better, to sharpen her own arguments when writing for the majority opinion.

They could see each other, not just as a political cut-out, but as a complete person.

Love doesn't mean we have to agree on everything. It means we listen more to our heart than to our head.

Scalia and Ginsburg knew how to do that. They often disagreed when it came to interpreting the law, but their hearts agreed on being friends.

There are things more important than votes, more important than winning or being right. Scalia and Ginsburg never lost sight of that simple truth: Love is more important than being right.

And who can blame them? Love is at the heart of any good friendship, but what happens when love is missing?

The Integrity Test – When Love is Missing

When I was twelve years old, I was walking to school, wearing my brand-new jeans. A group of girls I vaguely knew from school walked up to me and without addressing me directly, began commenting on my pants.

"Oh, those jeans are not at all out of fashion, are they?" began the leader.

"Oh, no, not at all," one of her pals chimed in.

My sense of fashion—or more precisely my lack thereof—was the continued conversation of the girls as we made our way to school. By the time we walked through the school doorway I felt ashamed and humiliated and was thoroughly disgusted with my new blue jeans.

Did I wear those jeans after that? Not a chance! And I still remember this more than four decades later.

To be clear, I'll readily admit to my poor sense of fashion at the time. I was wearing bell bottoms, which might have made a good fashion statement ten years earlier, but by the late 1970s they showed I was a tad out of touch.

The girls were making a point, and they weren't wrong. But when we're lording our superior knowledge—about fashion or any other topic—over another person, truth can be used as a tool to tear down rather than to build up. Love builds, but when we opt for power it's a clear sign that love is missing. Power tears people down.

Truth without love can be used as a weapon to shame and humiliate people. There's no integrity in that.

A lack of love for others is one side of the problem. When love is missing, power is quick to take its place. We may try to justify our actions by telling ourselves that *it's for the greater good*, or *the end justifies the means*. It's how we talk ourselves into doing something that our heart knows is wrong.

In extreme situations it is used to justify wars, the ultimate act of tribalism. It's us against them. We love our own tribe, but not those evildoers over there. It happens between countries, and it happens between groups within a country.

While a lack of respect for others is common, integrity also requires that we love and respect ourselves.

Like Daniel and Gina, we need to overcome the negative habits of our mind and emotions when feelings of fear and unworthiness take over. Shame, blame, fear and guilt are poisons that can keep us from finding the loving viewpoint inside our heart.

Finding that viewpoint isn't always easy; it takes a sustained effort to keep our heart open, and to value it and listen to it. When we do, it pays big dividends on the inner scorecard.

Better Than Anything I Could Have Ever Imagined

I've known Todd for over three decades. We don't see each other a lot, with him living in Chile, but it's always good to see him when I do. He's added some gray hair over the years, but what stands out most is that there's a calm and steadiness about him. It seems to say: I know who I am, and I am comfortable with who I am.

When I recently met him during one of his trips back to the U.S., I asked him how he'd been, and his answer caught me off guard.

"So much better than anything I could have ever imagined."

When I followed up with him later, I asked him to rate himself on the inner scorecard. He immediately went for eleven, twelve, thirteen, before settling on ten—because I wouldn't let him pick a higher number. If you don't know Todd you might think he is bragging, but he is not one to exaggerate. He truly loves his life.

But why? What has he done with his life that has made it so good?

The simple answer is that *he has made love the center of his life.*

Todd told me about a powerful moment that set him on his path when he was seventeen. His older sister passed away due to melanoma, a form of skin cancer.

During the funeral his grandfather broke down and yelled at God, "Why didn't you take me?" He was a religious man, but his faith had failed him, and this made a deep impression on Todd. "I decided right there and then that I would live a uniquely transcendent, powerful life, where I would have no regrets and that my faith would never fail me."

A powerful intention, that he carried through in the rest of his life.

Doing What You Love

In college as a psychology and art history major, he took a fiction writing workshop. The teacher recommended that he take a poetry workshop too. He knew nothing about poetry, but when he signed up, he discovered he loved it. He really felt a connection, both with the poetry and his teacher, and he began writing poetry. He won a writing contest, and doors began to open for him.

He ended up switching his major to writing and getting his degree in poetry from the University of Minnesota.

This unplanned switch was what he calls *spiritual serendipity*. While many of us might resist such a gentle nudge to move in a new direction, Todd embraced it. "I believe there's no such thing as an accident. We're always in the right place at the right time." He simply accepts it as life's way of moving him in a new and better direction that allowed him to be more in alignment with his talents and dreams.

Todd's life appears to be a succession of unplanned switches—he calls them portals—where something touches his heart, and he has the courage to follow it. Each portal took his life in a new direction, transporting him to a new reality, with new opportunities to grow.

The next portal opened up as he was finishing his degree at the University of Minnesota. He felt a deep connection with the writings of Pablo Neruda, a Chilean poet. While writing his thesis on Neruda's life, he became somewhat obsessed with the poet, and he felt a strong inner nudge telling him to pack up and move to Chile.

What was there for him in Chile? And was this really the right thing to do? He wasn't sure, so he asked for a sign, some confirmation that he was on the right track.

He was taking a Spanish class off campus from a Uruguayan writer. One day after class his teacher said, "Todd, there's a concert coming up. You've got to go to it. If you do one thing in your life, do this. It's a band from Chile, they're called Inti-Illiamani and they're so amazing."

Todd blew it off. Next week his teacher asked if he had bought tickets to the show yet. "No. I've been kind of busy," he said. His teacher became adamant, "Buy the tickets!" Todd was still not convinced. Another week went by, and he asked again, "Did you buy your tickets?" Todd admitted that he hadn't, and he decided to buy the tickets just so that his teacher would stop bugging him about it.

When he took his seat for the concert—he ended up with the last two seats in the last row—he had the most amazing experience he's had in his life. The music of this Chilean band touched his heart in a deep way, resolving any doubt he had about moving to Chile. He got his confirmation.

Protecting and Preserving What You Love

In Chile he ended up teaching North American literature at the university in the sleepy town of Valparaíso.

The more time he spent in Valparaíso, the more he fell in love with it, and a new dream began to ripen. What if he could find a way to make sure the beauty and culture of Valparaíso was preserved by making it a world heritage site?

After several years of teaching, he again chose to follow his dream. He created the Valparaíso Foundation, a non-profit dedicated to promoting the rebirth of Valparaíso as a cultural heritage site. He ran the foundation, which threw him into the world of fundraising, politics and advocacy. It also pushed him into the limelight. He became a public figure, which led to him having his share of admirers as well as local activists who couldn't stomach the idea that this non-native gringo was getting all the attention.

What he accomplished on behalf of Valparaíso couldn't be denied though. When the historic quarter of Valparaíso was declared a UNESCO world heritage site, his role in this was recognized. The local paper, *El Mercurio de Valparaíso,* invited him to write a column. Then the same paper nominated him as "Person of the Year" and Todd's star rose even higher when a documentary about his life was aired on public television.

He was highly respected and admired and had great influence in Valparaíso. He'd reached the pinnacle of success.

"But," he admits, "it was a very stressful time. The pressure was tremendous. I was a big deal in Valparaíso for twelve years, but it all hinged on me. The foundation had no endowment, no donors, nobody could do what I was doing."

He knew the Foundation couldn't survive without him, and yet his heart told him to walk away. So he made the decision to withdraw from the Foundation and from his public role in Valparaíso. The cycle had run its course, and it was time to make room for something new.

Serving What You Love

What came next took him by surprise. Since his early twenties, Todd has followed a spiritual teaching that is near and dear to his heart. This spiritual path gives its students the tools to grow into a state of spiritual freedom. Todd has a daily spiritual practice that has helped him to expand the awareness of his heart. These daily spiritual exercises allowed him to come into harmony with the Light and Sound, the two main aspects of Divine Spirit.

Todd loves his spiritual path.

When he received an offer to take on a new leadership role he was blown away. Would he be interested in becoming the main representative for these teachings in all of Chile? It would mean being responsible for coordinating all activities and volunteers within the country, no small task.

It didn't take him long to accept this new role and all the work and responsibilities that came with it.

With every step and new chapter in his life, he had the opportunity to do something he loved while at the same time expanding his capacity for love.

After stepping away from his role in Valparaíso, Todd found a new home in Patagonia, the southern part of Chile. He lives on a fabulous property, against the backdrop of the mountains, with his family and a growing menagerie of horses, llamas and other animals.

"Some people misunderstand why I'm so happy," he told me. "They think life is so good because I have a beautiful farm. But the truth is that I love my life because I've dedicated the last thirty-five years of my life to sanctifying and beautifying my state of consciousness. The farm is just a reflection of that.

"We think we find success because we pursue it. Not so," says Todd. He observes that "The less we need success, materially, emotionally and intellectually, the more it pursues us. We serve life through our state of consciousness. The happier we are living in our state of consciousness, the more success finds us."

Todd's focus for the last few decades has been to beautify and sanctify his state of consciousness, and he credits the inner qualities he's cultivated through his spiritual practice for his success. To put it another way, he has made love the center of his life and of his being. That's the reason for his success.

The Tree of Love

While for many of us love conjures up the image of a couple in love, holding hands and staring into each other's eyes, romantic love is just one aspect of love. Love shows up in any meaningful relationship. Parent and child, brothers and sisters, friendships, pets, we can love the work we do, or a hobby we enjoy. For some of us love extends to loving God, ourselves, and every living thing.

Love is the inner act of caring, and it has an effect.

Paul O'Neill cared about the people at Alcoa and he cared about the people employed by the U.S. Treasury. Chiune Sugihara cared about the Jews that were caught in a terrible war and looking for safety. Richard and Oracene Williams cared about their children, giving them the best start they could in life. Jill Taylor cared about rebuilding her brain and her life. Walter Williams cared about the children who needed a helping hand. Tom cared about his wife and about healing the connection with her family. Warren Buffett cared about making money and playing the investment game.

In all cases, love was the guiding force that drove them to make things better.

I see love as a tree. The trunk represents love, the branches the many ways in which love expresses itself in the world and in our lives.

For Paul O'Neill, protecting people from harm was a branch. For Sugihara, following his conscience and showing respect to every Jewish refugee was a branch. For the Williams family, raising children with awesome tennis skills and a champion-mindset was a branch. For Tom, taking full responsibility for himself and his life was a branch.

Love can take many forms. But it has to be inside you first. That was Todd's secret. For decades he worked on strengthening the love inside him. His success with poetry, teaching, leading a foundation and then taking a leadership role in his spiritual path were the natural fruits.

Once love is inside of you, it has to come out, and it will try to make things better. It will serve others, protect, beautify, teach, heal, strengthen and if needed, rebuild, but never by forcing our will on someone else.

It drives us to be self-disciplined and strive for excellence.

It comes out as responsibility, kindness, grace and respect. When we have love inside, a moral compass is not something we learn, it is something we listen to and act on, perception and action.

Summary

- Love is a measure of how much we care, and it aims to make things better.

- The heart of any good relationship is love. Love finds a way to see beyond our differences.

- The more we make love a priority and expand our capacity for love, the higher our score on the inner scorecard.

- Three obstacles we need to overcome to gain love:
  - Power problem–the lust for power, a desire to dominate and control others.
  - Fear problem–fear closes the heart, cutting us off from love. It takes courage to face our fears.
  - Opinion problem–while shame and guilt keep us from being able to accept love, hatred and anger keep

us from giving love to others.

- Love is an essential element of integrity. When we shame, blame, guilt or otherwise try to control others we are not treating them with the love and respect they deserve, and we have lost integrity.

- Love can take many forms. It motivates us to serve others and is the basis of our moral compass. It comes out as responsibility, kindness, grace and respect.

Chapter 11

Sorting Fact from Fiction

If you don't read the newspaper, you are uninformed. If you do read the newspaper, you are mis-informed.

—Mark Twain

Quote: Modern flat Earth beliefs are promoted by organizations and individuals advocating that the Earth is flat while denying the Earth's sphericity, contrary to over two millennia of scientific consensus.
Source: Wikipedia.

Let's begin with acknowledging that there is a group of people, here in the 21st century, who believe the earth is flat. They have conferences where they get together to discuss the flatness of the earth and expound on the different reasons why they are right and everyone else is wrong. Contrary to what you might think, this group is much larger than you would imagine.

It's easy to shrug your shoulders and think: *Some people will believe anything* and move on. But I love the spirit of this group.

To be clear, I don't believe the Earth is flat, but I do believe we have something important to learn about the nature of truth from these contrarians.

What Is Truth?

Truth is reality, regardless of what you think, what I think, and what the scientific consensus is. Truth simply is what it is. We may agree with it or not. It doesn't matter. Truth is truth. We can discover truth and realize truth.

You may be the only person in the world who has discovered it. You may be shunned and shamed because the consensus of scientists is that you're wrong, but you will still be right.

This was the fate of Dan Shechtman. His research during the 1980s into metallic crystals led him to believe there were quasicrystals that had a repeating but non-symmetrical structure. This put him at odds with the entire scientific community, who in unison shamed him for his heretical beliefs. (Yes, science does at times behave just like a religion.) Two-time Nobel laureate Linus Pauling was quoted as saying: "There is no such thing as quasicrystals, only quasi-scientists."

The head of Shechtman's research group didn't take too kindly to his findings either, telling him to "go back and read the textbook" before asking him to leave for "bringing disgrace on the team."

You have to love human nature. We can be so sure of ourselves, especially when we are part of the consensus. When everyone agrees with us, and we agree with everyone else who matters, it's easy to fall for the lure of consensus. Consensus makes us lose our humility and curiosity, two essential elements of the proper attitude for conducting inquiries into the nature of reality.

Shechtman was not deterred and published his paper anyway. As other scientists started duplicating his findings, the tide began to shift. His final moment of victory was when he was awarded the Nobel Prize in Chemistry in 2011 for exactly this discovery.

In the 1980s the consensus in the scientific community was that Dan Shechtman was a fraud. Today the scientific consensus is that he's a brilliant scientist. If anything, it should show us that consensus is no reliable indicator of the truth. Scientists are human, and like the rest of us, sometimes they get it right, and sometimes they get it wrong.

Truth is reality and the reality is that our world has order. It takes a special interest, curiosity, and talent, to suss out the timeless principles that create this order.

Once we grasp these principles, we begin to understand how things work. It puts the power in our hands to create a better future. It also puts the power in our hands to destroy that future. This is the double-edged sword of truth.

Seeing Things As They Are?

We often take it for granted that we see things as they are, but there are forces at work, both inside and outside us, that distort our perception of reality. It takes effort on our part to see through these distortions—illusions—that keep us from seeing reality clearly.

In today's world, news articles go out of their way to refer to the scientific consensus. It should make you think. It's a subtle cue that encourages you to stop thinking for yourself, adopt the view of the consensus, and shelve your curiosity. It's a done deal. People much smarter than you have already gone over this. No need for you to think for yourself. There is already a scientific consensus. And we all know that scientists are the smartest people of all.

It encourages orthodoxy—the forming of an established belief that should not and in many cases is not allowed to be questioned.

I'm not saying that the consensus opinion of scientists is always wrong. It may very well be right. But we shouldn't confuse it with the scientific process or the truth. It's an *opinion*. Sometimes our opinions take us for a ride, and we forget that. And that presumes that there really is a scientific consensus. Scientists are much like the rest of us—there usually is a wide range of opinions, so a true consensus is not all that common.

I am a strong believer in the right of every individual to form their own opinion. In fact, I would go a step further and say it's our duty to form our own opinions, in a deliberate and thoughtful way. But too often our opinions are the result of lazy thinking or no thinking at all. We all engage in lazy thinking from time to time. There's only so much time in the day, so we go for the shortcut. We're only human.

Here are three common shortcuts that I'm pretty sure we've all used at one time or another.

1. Other people believe it.

Psychologists call this social proof. The more people believe something to be true, the stronger our belief that it is true. It is an easy shortcut when we ourselves have little knowledge of it. For instance, when there are two restaurants next to each other, one is full, while the other has barely any people in it. If you have eaten in both restaurants, you have your own opinion, based on your own experience, and you're not likely to be swayed by the large group of people in the first restaurant. But if you haven't experienced the food in either restaurant you will almost certainly be swayed by social proof and feel that the restaurant with all the people in it has the better food.

2. Authority.

When someone in a position of authority tells us this is the truth, we tend to believe them. Doctors are a great example. If you ever read an article on health, notice how the reporter nearly always quotes a doctor's opinion. Doctors are often portrayed with a white coat and a stethoscope loosely draped over their shoulders. These props reinforce their authority. They tell us: here is someone who knows what she's talking about. Here again we substitute someone else's opinion or belief for our own experience. It's a shortcut we use to form an opinion in absence of doing the work to form our own opinion based on our experience and the best available evidence.

3. Repetition.

The most egregious way in which we adopt beliefs out of laziness is repetition. We believe things because we've heard them repeated many times. The mere fact that we hear an opinion or belief repeated makes us believe it's true, sometimes in spite of having our own experience to the contrary. This is the basis of propaganda. Joseph Goebbels, Hitler's chief propagandist, said: "If you repeat a lie often enough, people will believe it, and you will even come to believe it yourself."

Repetition works, but for it to become an effective propaganda tool it needs its partner, censorship, to suppress any information that contradicts it.

Many news outlets and pundits that aim to tell us what to believe and disbelieve have turned themselves into propaganda centers. They filter and censor information, removing context to promote a specific agenda. They generally use these three shortcuts to their advantage and are quite effective at controlling our beliefs.

The words "scientific consensus" automatically invoke the first two shortcuts. Scientists are the experts, the authority. The consensus means that not only do other people believe it, but practically all of them believe it and all of them are experts. That's a lot of authority. It feels mighty lonely to form an opinion that goes against that. Even more so if it is repeated over and over again.

We are all susceptible to these shortcuts because they're easy. When we don't discipline ourselves, we do what's easy, because that's what comes naturally. But very few things worth having come without effort, and truth is no exception.

The good part is that once you recognize these shortcuts you can start building up your immunity to them. You can form your opinions consciously and gather information and arguments on both sides of the issue.

There's a reason why in a court of law there's a prosecutor, a judge and a lawyer for the defense. The judge is there to make sure that both sides can present their case. And both sides will present experts that will have widely varying and often opposing opinions. And that puts the ball right back where it belongs, in your court.

Your beliefs, your truth. How much do you care about them? If you care enough, you will take responsibility for separating facts from fiction.

This is what I think the flat-Earthers understand and get right, while many of us round-Earthers get it wrong. They care enough about truth not to take the shortcuts. They're not outsourcing their right to determine what's true by simply believing the Earth is round because so many others believe it, or because an authority tells them. Integrity doesn't always mean you get it right, but it means you have to care enough about truth to find the best arguments and make up your own mind.

Dan Shechtman was like a flat-Earther when he discovered this new crystalline structure that was unknown at the time. It was him against the whole world. He could have bowed to the pressure. It would have been easier, but it would have been wrong on many levels. Why? His integrity demanded it. He cared enough about the truth to stand up for it.

Choosing our beliefs, our truth, consciously and carefully is not usually the easy road, but in the end, it is the only road worth taking.

The Map

From the moment we are born, we begin to build *the map*.

I call it the map because I don't know what else to call it. It's all the knowledge and beliefs we carry around in our mind about anything and everything. Some of it is literally a map that tells us how to get from here to there. Some of it is what foods and vitamins our bodies need to stay healthy and what toxic substances we need to stay away from. It's all the knowledge we've accumulated about ourselves and the world around us. To say it scientifically, it's a map of where things are, how things are, why things are and how things work.

To keep it interesting the map not only contains our knowledge, it also contains how we feel about it. About people, places and things, including ourselves.

The map covers everything from God and our place in the universe to how to play tic-tac-toe. It's the model we build in our mind to help us navigate the world.

The good news is that the map works pretty well to manage our day-to-day activities. The bad news is that our map is riddled with errors and has giant holes in it. It's a model. Even though it works well enough for routine activities, it will never be 100% accurate or complete. Which means that there will always be situations in which it doesn't work well at all.

The Web of Illusion

To understand truth we need to also understand what's keeping us from seeing truth clearly: the forces of illusion.

The forces of illusion are always hard at work to distort the way we see reality. If you look at figure 11.1 it seems as if there is a black dot moving around. As soon as you look at a different part of the grid the original black dot seems to disappear while you see the black dot in a new place. The most I've been able to see at the same time are two black dots if I focus in between the dots. But there are twelve black dots. Our mind simply will not let us see them all at once. It's an illusion built into the way we perceive the world. In figure 11.1 the gridlines are dominating our vision, making it so that all dots except the one we focus on seem to disappear. In figure 11.2 I removed the gridlines—the web of illusion—so we can see all the dots.

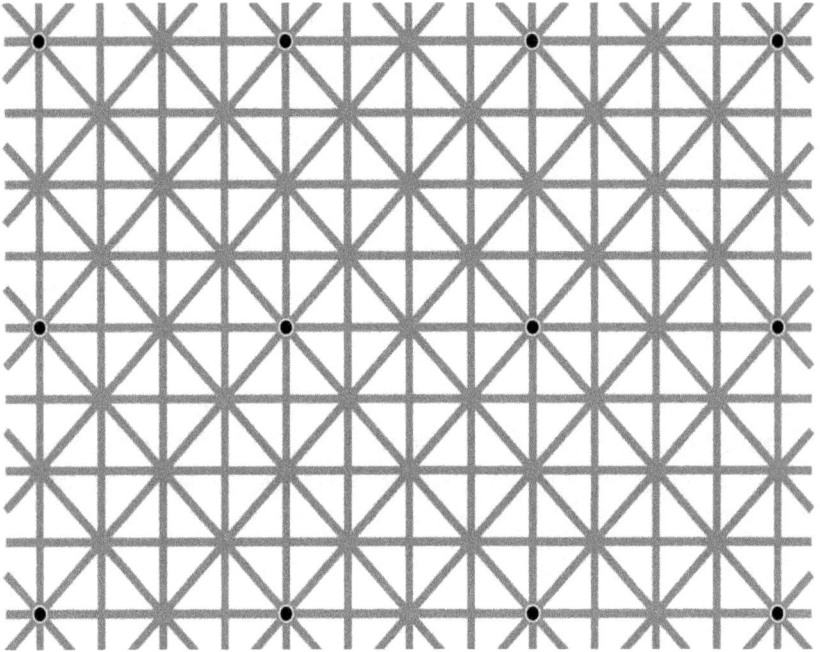

Figure 11.1

We see the world as much with our mind as with our eyes.

Our mind does not have the capacity to see the fullness of truth, so it creates a focus. This focus is our dominant belief system, the black dot. Our dominant belief system creates gridlines that filter our perception.

Our mind decides how to interpret what our eyes capture. Our interpretation is based on the belief that the pattern of gridlines is consistent, and therefore it filters out the other dots in figure 1. It's how the mind works. It refuses to let us see things that do not conform with a dominant or existing belief. The mind believes the gridlines are following a consistent pattern, so that's what we see.

The mind interprets, massages and overrides what our eyes see to make it conform with our map.

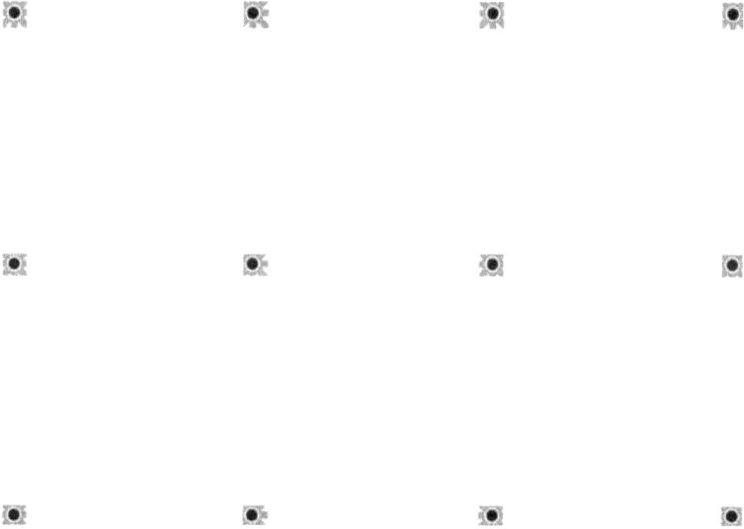

Figure 11.2

Some Eastern religions call this maya—illusion. It's the notion that we lack the ability to see reality clearly. It's not our fault, it's just that the mind is a bit wonky and easily tricked into believing all kinds of things. In fact, in the absence of an existing belief, the mind will gladly make one up.

Psychologists know about the confirmation bias—the tendency of our mind to seek out and interpret information that confirms our existing beliefs. The optical illusion in figure 11.1 is the confirmation bias in action.

The web of gridlines is really a web of illusion. And it operates not just when we are looking at this picture, but it does so all the time, usually without us being aware of it. In our everyday life, the gridlines are created by our beliefs about reality. These beliefs create expectations, filter out information and shape our perception.

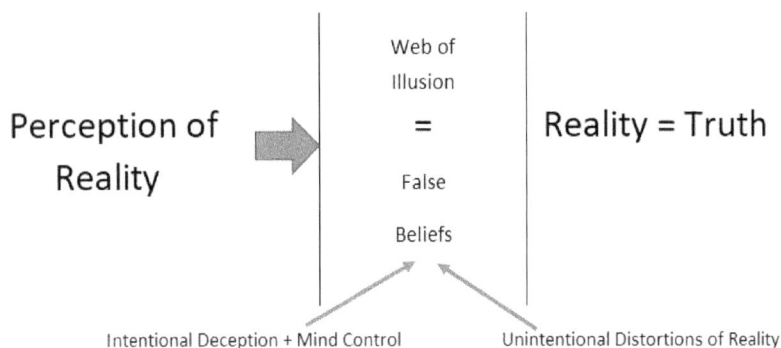

Figure 11.3

It may seem like a big jump from not being able to see the dots because of the gridlines to believing that our whole perception of reality is off. Most of us would prefer to think that our map is perfect. We have no false beliefs; therefore, we see reality exactly as it is.

Psychologists would disagree. They've mapped a number of mechanisms that lead to significant biases in our perception. In a famous experiment a person in a gorilla suit walks onto a basketball court while a group of people is passing the ball around. A group of subjects were asked to count how many times the ball was passed around in the court. Half of them didn't see the person in the gorilla suit. That's attentional bias. Once again, the mind shows it's perfectly capable of filtering out information that we're seeing with our own eyes.

We also touched on the confirmation bias, our mind's tendency to selectively seek, remember and focus on information that confirms our existing beliefs, while filtering out things that are inconsistent with the beliefs in our map.

I think you get the point. Our beliefs, whether true or false, affect directly how we see the world and the choices we make. The better our map, the better we are able to make choices. But our map has some inevitable inaccuracies—false beliefs.

How We Acquire False Beliefs

So where do these false beliefs come from?

Oddly enough, some of our beliefs are simply assumptions. Whenever there's an ambiguous situation, the mind tries to fill in the missing information and make it unambiguous. The mind doesn't usually tell us when it's making an assumption. Whenever there's a hole in our knowledge, the mind makes a guess and happily assumes that guess is the truth.

I caught my mind doing this once while I was waiting behind a pickup truck at an intersection. It was a four-way stop and there was one other car at the intersection. The other car went first and cleared the intersection. There were no other cars, but the truck didn't move.

I believed the driver was probably on his phone, not paying attention to the fact that the intersection was clear. So I honked my horn. The truck still didn't move. I was about to honk again, this time putting a little more umph into it, when I saw an elderly lady with a cane slowly crossing the street. She had been blocked from my view by the truck in front of me.

Only then did I realize how my mind had seamlessly inserted the belief that the driver in the pickup truck was distracted. The mind can be an awesome tool, but it has its drawbacks. This is one of them.

Then there are the deliberate lies.

The Integrity Code

The three most common reasons why people lie.

1. *Because they want to hide their own shortcomings.*
   Who hasn't done this? It's all too human to lie about ourselves because we want others to have a positive opinion about us. Underneath this lie sits a fear. What would people do if they knew the truth about me? We're scared that we'll be rejected when others know the truth about us. Better not to take the risk and present a more "perfect" picture, even if it isn't true.

2. *Because they believe the lie will lead to personal gain, or the truth will lead to personal loss.*
   Famous examples are men like Bernie Madoff and Lance Armstrong. They both amassed sizable amounts of money and in Lance's case, fame. For some people personal gain is about power. When politicians lie it's often because they want to gain power and keep it of course. Lies seem like a small price to pay for such a prize.

3. *Because they are under the spell of illusion and believe something that isn't true.*
   To be fair, this isn't a deliberate lie, but rather how lies get perpetuated. People who are honest and sincere, once convinced of a lie, can become true proponents, even though their sincere belief is based on a lie. This is perhaps the worst of the three. These people can be quite convincing because they are so sincere. They are true believers. But, how strongly we feel about our belief being true is no indication of its actual truthfulness.

The world is full of lies and misinformation. Some of it intentional, some of it unintentional.

This is not necessarily a bad thing, but it is something we have to acknowledge and deal with. The sooner we do, the more likely we are to get on with separating fact from fiction.

People believe what they believe, often because they feel strongly that it is true. However, the strength of our feeling is not a valid substitute for having good discrimination. One of the benefits of age and experience is that it gives us time to finetune our senses and learn to discriminate between truth and illusion. But it takes effort and curiosity, and the humility to admit we were wrong.

Developing a keen eye for the truth means we have to develop the ability to see through the lies and illusions that are all around us. And that means we have to challenge our own beliefs from time to time. Because we all have beliefs that are false, either in part or completely so[8].

Beliefs that are ingrained in a group become part of the culture. It usually takes someone from the outside to perceive this and call it out. This is what Paul O'Neill did when he became CEO of Alcoa. He challenged the belief that accidents in the workplace are inevitable and acceptable. By doing so he challenged, and eventually changed, the culture of the organization.

Integrity implies a willingness to stay open to new information and ideas, even if that challenges our existing beliefs. It is good to challenge our beliefs. Integrity requires us to stay open to new information and update our beliefs when new evidence shows up.

This is hard. It's human nature to resist new information, especially when it clashes with our existing beliefs.

---

[8] If you think you are the exception to the rule, I encourage you to challenge yourself. You can test your global knowledge at factfulnessquiz.com, based on the book *Factfulness* by Hans Rosling, and see if you can score better than a monkey.

The Integrity Test – Salty Laundry

When I was a little boy I wanted to help my mother. I had seen her put up laundry and cooking meat in the kitchen. I was determined to help out. But I got mixed up about what white powder would go where, and I ended up putting laundry detergent on the meat and salt in the laundry machine.

I was so young that I have no memory of it, but the story was told and retold so many times that it became a solid part of my history.

Little sprout that I was, I was intent on helping out. My intentions were good (love). But I was unable to translate those intentions into the right actions.

It's adorable when this happens to a four-year-old—at least my parents seemed to think so—but not quite as adorable when it happens on a grander scale.

I think of it as the Salty Laundry problem, but people have observed this problem long before I messed up our family's dinner. It has its own proverb: *The road to hell is paved with good intentions*. It's why good intentions are not enough.

The Law of Unintended Consequences is triggered when our heart is in the right place, but our understanding of how things work is limited. We don't see the full picture, and therefore our actions end up causing unintended problems.

Besides the Salty Laundry problem, which deals with unintended consequences, there are also deliberate lies. In a worst-case scenario these can be disseminated and perpetuated through censorship and propaganda.

Countries like Russia and China have well known mind-control programs in place using censorship and propaganda.

Even in the U.S. where freedom of speech and freedom of the press is enshrined in the constitution, propaganda and censorship have become part and parcel of our daily life. It's par for the course.

It takes some effort even here to find the truth, especially on subjects which have been politicized.

It comes back to this: We can't outsource our search for truth. We have to do our due diligence. And that means finding people we can trust, who report on events without a censorship or propaganda filter, or, barring that, finding people presenting viewpoints with different ideological backgrounds. We have to look for the best available information and then form our opinion based on that.

In this respect people who have moved to the U.S. from either China or Russia are much more likely to have closed the authority gap. They don't necessarily believe the experts on TV because they know how the game is played. It's second nature to them to question authority and rely on their own ability to discern the truth. Those of us who grew up in the West often still believe that we don't have a censorship and propaganda problem.

Many politicians have been known to take full advantage of this.

The Bush administration started a war against Iraq based on the belief that Saddam Hussein had weapons of mass destruction. Whether it was an honest mistake, or a calculated deception used as a pretext we may never know for sure. But as Paul O'Neill pointed out, it would be madness to start a war based on such grainy pictures.

Bush as the Commander in Chief went with the grainy pictures anyway—calling them evidence—and used them to swing public opinion towards support for the war. The weapons were of course never found.

Champions for Truth

Ignaz Semmelweis, a 19th century Hungarian physician, discovered that death due to childbed fever, now known to be caused by a bacterial infection, could be significantly reduced when the attending physicians washed their hands.

He noticed that wards using midwives had much lower mortality rates than those that were serviced by physicians. In those days physicians were known to go directly from cutting into dead bodies to helping women deliver their babies.

When he instituted hand washing with a chlorinated lime solution the mortality rate plummeted in the doctors' wards. He assumed hand washing eliminated something the physicians carried on their hands, but he couldn't prove what it was. The germ theory had not yet been fleshed out.

Even though he published his findings, doctors around the country simply ignored his advice. Why did they ignore it when the data were so convincing? Wards that implemented the hand washing went from a mortality rate of almost 20% to less than 2%.

This was a couple centuries ago, and maybe people were not as smart then and they didn't have the internet. But consider Carole Baggerly, who in today's world, even with the internet, has been waging a very similar uphill battle.

As a breast cancer patient, she received the standard treatment: chemo and radiation. After this ordeal she was astounded to find out that there was a large scientific body of research that showed there was a very strong link between vitamin D blood levels and the chance of getting cancer as well as long-term survival after cancer.

Why didn't her doctors tell her this? Appalled by the gap between what vitamin D researchers know and what doctors tell their patients, she took action.

In 2007 she started GrassrootsHealth, a non-profit dedicated to doing research into the effects of vitamin D and other micro-nutrients on our health. She's been making this research available to people and medical providers around the world ever since.

As noted on the grassrootshealth.net website, multiple research studies found that vitamin D blood levels of 60 ng/ml can reduce the risk of breast cancer by 80% or more. That's not insignificant if you consider that one in eight women will be diagnosed with breast cancer some time in their life.

That's an astounding level of prevention, and it's only the tip of the iceberg when it comes to vitamin D. If only half of the claims on the website are true—and there are at least fifty scientists associated with the organization who have staked their reputation on it—then getting vitamin D blood levels up to functional levels would cause a health revolution.

Carole has come to appreciate what a monumental task it is to educate people on a single aspect of truth: Our bodies need vitamin D, and most people need more than they get from food and make from exposure to the sun. Could we cut the cost of health care in this country in half if everyone had sufficient vitamin D in their blood? Who knows? The data seem to point in that direction, so Carole[9] and her staff at GrassrootsHealth keep plugging away at their mission of educating people.

Like Semmelweiss, she's discovered that sharing her wisdom isn't easy. Resistance to truth is a condition built in to us. It's human nature.

Most people are passive about truth, which is the sure way to stay stuck in your existing beliefs. It takes an active approach to pierce the web of illusion. It takes thinking for yourself. It takes curiosity and effort to seek out information that does not match your existing viewpoints and beliefs. It takes self-reflection and honesty, asking yourself: *Have I been falling back on the shortcuts of authority, social proof and repetition?*

It takes self-discipline to develop the ability to discriminate between what's true and what's not.

When we do, and we can see truth more clearly, there is a payoff: being able to make better decisions.

---

[9] Carole Baggerly passed away on October 26, 2024, at age 82, almost twenty years after being diagnosed with breast cancer.

Enter Charlie Munger and Warren Buffett.

Buffett and Munger

When Charlie and Warren met it was love at first sight, although not of the romantic kind. They were perhaps most in love with each other's minds. Although on a lunch date with two other couples, Charlie and Warren seemed oblivious to everyone else as they discussed investing—Warren's very favorite subject. When the other couples left it's unclear if Charlie and Warren noticed, they were so engrossed in their conversation.

Charlie was a lawyer, making his living in Los Angeles, while Warren had set up shop in Omaha, where he was managing the money for the people who invested in his partnership. Delighted by this new friendship, Charlie and Warren continued their conversations on the phone with increasing frequency.

It was the beginning of a lifelong friendship, that in time expanded into a business partnership. By that time Charlie was deep into investing as well, and it made sense for them to merge their businesses together under the umbrella of Berkshire Hathaway.

Berkshire was one of Warren's early investments, a textile company, that never gave him the return on investment he had hoped for. But rather than selling it off, he turned Berkshire into the holding company for all the companies that he invested in.

Warren and Charlie are masters of perception. They put their preconceived notions aside and set out to understand better than anyone else which companies would make good investments. A matter of seeing truth more clearly and therefore being able to make better investment decisions.

The difference it made for them was beyond huge.

According to data from Business Insider, $100 invested in the S&P500 in 1964 would have grown to a healthy $5000 by 2014.

But the same amount invested in Berkshire Hathaway would have netted you more than $1,000,000. Over a span of fifty years Buffett and Munger outperformed the S&P500 by more than 200x.

Buffett and Munger were able to have such incredible results because they were able to see and recognize truth more clearly than practically any other investor.

Summary

- Truth is reality—the world we live in. Our understanding of reality is our map. The map contains everything we know and believe to be true about everything, ourselves included. Our map is a model, and therefore always incomplete.

- It's easy to introduce false beliefs to our map when we rely on shortcuts like social proof, authority and repetition.

- Illusions—false beliefs—are self-perpetuating because they act as perceptual filters. There is no easy way to get rid of illusions. It takes curiosity, effort and humility on our part.

- There is no alternative to developing our personal discrimination. Right discrimination allows us to discover and replace false beliefs.

- From time-to-time champions for truth come along to challenge existing orthodoxies. The challenge is to recognize them as they often go unnoticed by the crowds.

Chapter 12

30,000 Brushstrokes

For to be free is not merely to cast off one's chains, but to live in a way that respects and enhances the freedom of others.
—Nelson Mandela

The Journey to Freedom

Freddie was born in Maryland in the early 1800s to a black woman. He had few memories of his mother, because slave babies were separated from their mother soon after birth. But she did come to visit him on a few occasions, when she could make the twelve-mile journey by foot, and back, before the next day started.

Fred was initially raised by his grandma, until, at six years old, he was deemed old enough to move to the big house where his "old master" lived. His main hardships as a boy were being cold and underfed. With few clothes, no blanket to sleep under, and a slave woman named Aunt Katy who dispensed the food to the children, he suffered from cold and lack of food. Aunt Katy had a cruel streak, and she decided to punish Fred—for something he was not even aware of having done—by starving him.

As a child he witnessed the brutality of the slave system. Owners had overseers who would enforce discipline with regular whippings. But owners themselves could use the lash too when the mood struck them.

Two slaves—Esther and Edward—were in love. But Captain Anthony, Esther's owner, for some reason disapproved of their courtship, and forbade them to meet. The young lovers would not stay apart, and Captain Anthony punished Esther by tying her up and then using a cowhide whip on her back and shoulders. "Again and again, he drew the hateful scourge through his hand, adjusting it with a view of dealing the most pain-giving blow his strength and skill could inflict."

The shock of seeing this was tremendous. Fred was "terrified, hushed, stunned and bewildered," and yet he saw this scene repeated numerous times, because the two lovers continued to meet.

Baltimore

Things became a lot better for him when he was sent to Baltimore to live with Mr. and Mrs. Hugh Auld where he was to take care of their son Thomas. Fred was especially taken with Mrs. Auld who had a kind, gentle and cheerful disposition. He now received enough to eat and good clean clothes and was mostly running errands and making sure little Tommy stayed out of harm's way.

Freddie frequently saw Mrs. Auld read the Bible out loud, and he asked her to teach him to read. She began teaching him, and he soon mastered the alphabet and spelling small words. But once she told Mr. Auld how well Freddie was progressing, he told her to stop teaching him, which she did.

As he explained to his wife, it was not only against the law; it was also unsafe. "Learning will spoil the best nigger in the world. If he learns to read the Bible, it will forever unfit him to be a slave. He should know nothing but the will of his master and learn to obey it."

It was a moment of revelation to Fred, who had struggled to understand why the white man was able to perpetuate the enslavement of the black man. Mr. Auld made it clear that knowledge was a key difference between slaves and free men. It showed him how to move forward on the pathway from slavery to freedom. Learning how to read would allow him to gain more knowledge.

Mrs. Auld, now duly instructed by her husband, no longer taught Freddie. She even became angry when she saw him read a book or newspaper. But Fred was undeterred, and he took it upon himself to continue his learning. Whenever he was sent on an errand or was allowed playtime, he would use his time to learn. He asked his white playmates to teach him, or he looked up words in the Webster's spelling book he had gotten hold of.

This young boy would not let anything stop him from learning to read and write, skills that helped set him on the path to freedom.

Another notable influence to come into his life in Baltimore was Charles Lawson. He found in Uncle Lawson a spiritual role model and tutor that helped shape his views on religion. He spent as much of his free time with Lawson as he could and considered him his spiritual father. Lawson, a black man, encouraged him to cast all his cares upon God. This, after some struggle, he was able to do. As a result, he finally found his burden lightened and his heart relieved. "I loved all mankind, slaveholders not excepted, though I abhorred slavery more than ever."

How could this be? He was able to love slaveholders, but he hated slavery. How could the two be reconciled? He saw the negative effects the institution of slavery had on both the slaves and the slaveowners and recognized it for what it was: a corrupt system.

"A man's character always takes its hue, more or less, from the form and color of things about him. The slaveholder, as well as the slave, was the victim of the slave system. Under the whole heavens there could be no relation more unfavorable to the development of honorable character than that sustained by the slaveholder to the slave. Reason is imprisoned here, and passions run wild."

This deeply spiritual view allowed him to feel charity towards the ones who kept him enslaved.

The Negro Breaker

As Fred grew into a young man, he had to leave Baltimore and now serve his new master Thomas Auld. Thomas had married Lucretia, the daughter of Captain Anthony, and after the captain passed away, Fred became his property.

But things did not go well for Fred. He did not like his new master's character and his tendency to defend himself against his master's complaints caused a problem. Master Thomas decided that city life had ruined his slave and that he needed to be "broken."

Edward Covey had a reputation for being able to break young negroes. At seventeen years old Fred was sent to Covey to be broken. He received a steady diet of lashings and was worked so hard that he was always exhausted. He felt broken in body and spirit.

One day he fell sick, with an aching head and exhaustion, for which Covey beat him with a stick. Frederick decided to go see Master Thomas, his owner, to ask him to intercede for him. He hoped that if he wouldn't do so out of humanity, he would do it out of selfish reasons, for a slave was valuable, and a dead slave was worth nothing.

However, he received no help from Master Thomas and had no other option than to go back to Mr. Covey.

Before he returned, he made a decision, "For I had brought my mind to a firm resolve during that Sunday's reflection to obey every order, however unreasonable, if it were possible, and if Mr. Covey should then undertake to beat me to defend and protect myself to the best of my ability."

While obeying Covey's order to feed the horses and get them ready, Covey sneaked up on him and tried to tie him up. Fred had had enough, and he defended himself. He fought Covey for two hours. Covey, now as tired as Frederick, finally let go of him and told him to go to work. He had not been able to punish Frederick.

Frederick wasn't quite sure why he was never held to account for his actions. The law in Maryland was clear: A slave who resisted his master could be hanged. It was common for slaves who resisted to be publicly flogged to deter other slaves from following their example. None of that happened, perhaps because Covey did not want word to get out that he had been bested by a seventeen-year-old slave.

It was a turning point for Frederick. He had resisted and fought back. "It rekindled in my breast the smoldering embers of liberty," he said. It also changed his relationship with Covey. Never again did the man lay a hand on him in anger, and he served out the remaining six months of his term there without any more whippings.

Freedom

When he was next hired out to a much kinder master, Mr. Freeland, thoughts of escaping to freedom began to dominate his thinking again.

With five of his close friends, he came up with a plan to escape. On the day the escape was to take place the worst thing happened: They were betrayed. Soon, all of them were hauled off to prison, but as there was no proof other than one person's word that they were planning to escape, they were not sold into the deep south which was the usual result when slaves were caught trying to escape.

His friends were released first, and after a delay, he too was set free. But his master felt there was a lot of distrust and animosity towards him in the area, so instead of putting him to work in the fields, he sent him back to Baltimore, once again under the care of his brother, Mr. Hugh Auld.

There Frederick worked in the shipyards and learned a trade, which made him even more valuable. It also put his dream of escaping to freedom within reach. After making decent wages and each week having to turn them over to Mr. Auld, he finally took the long-awaited, and much anticipated leap to freedom. With the help of a document that certified he was a free American sailor he boarded a train going north. Even though the document wasn't his, and close scrutiny would have made that clear, it was an official document, and the conductor gave it only a glance. Nor did he encounter anyone challenging his right to travel as he made his way to Philadelphia and then New York.

Free at last!

Frederick Douglass went on to a career as a speaker and a printer, dedicating himself to the cause of educating people about slavery and to rid the country of its presence.

He even went on to meet with President Lincoln during the Civil War, urging him to give black soldiers equal pay and equal treatment. Lincoln listened to him and ordered that black soldiers be treated the same as the white men who had enlisted.

For most of us, our challenges pale in comparison with the challenges Frederick faced. There was no doubt a certain amount of luck involved in his gamble to escape from bondage. But he also instinctively seemed to embody the heart qualities of responsibility, resolve and resilience.

Responsibility

Responsibility is simple: It means we take responsibility for the choices we make and the way our life unfolds as a result. There will always be forces outside of our control. That was true then, and it is true today. But that doesn't mean we're not responsible for doing everything in our power to improve our life. This includes choosing a direction, choosing to invest in yourself, and choosing the teachers that can help you grow.

Choose a direction.

As Yogi Berra's timeless quote tells us, *If you don't know where you're going, you might end up somewhere else.*

Our first responsibility is to choose a direction, and our direction is based on our values. Even if you don't know exactly where you want to go, you can still choose a direction.

In the big picture there are only two directions: towards integrity, which is based on the values of love, truth and freedom, or the corruption of the ego, which includes shame, blame, fear, vanity and a lust for power.

In Frederick's case it was his strong desire for freedom that was part of choosing his direction. He chose freedom and love. He could have easily chosen bitterness and anger, but he chose love.

Choose to invest in yourself.

It is our responsibility to invest in ourselves and that means actively seeking out ways to grow our skills and knowledge.

Frederick asked to be taught so he could learn how to read. When Mrs. Auld stopped teaching him, he continued on his own. He invested in himself. He used his limited spare time to build his skills, very consciously and with determination. He taught himself to write with the help of a book and some of his white playmates.

When he made some money shining shoes, he used the money to buy himself "The Columbian Orator," a popular schoolbook. He was determined to educate himself.

No matter our age, the benefits of learning continue. Learning can and should be a part of life at every stage. By investing in ourselves we grow our agency, and agency is the key to more freedom.

Choose teachers to help you grow.

Beyond our early years as a child, we are responsible for choosing our role models and teachers. It is our responsibility to find *good* teachers. Not just any teacher will do. If we choose a teacher or role model who teaches us that hate or power is the answer, the fault is entirely our own.

There are good and bad teachers. It's our responsibility to develop the discrimination to know the difference. The clearer you are about your direction and your values, the easier it is to see if a particular teacher can help you or not.

Frederick had plenty of role models to choose from, and who did he pick? Uncle Lawson, a spiritual role model who showed him the importance of love and a spiritual mindset.

Resolve

Resolve is the ability to commit yourself to a course of action and to follow through. For some of us this is hard.

Resolve allows us to overcome the resistance inside us. There may be fear, laziness, and a number of other reasons not to follow through.

Before he fought Mr. Covey, Frederick made a resolution. He resolved to follow any reasonable order, and to defend himself if Covey tried to punish him for no reason. It was a resolution that could have cost him his life, but he did it anyway. It was a matter of self-respect.

Resolve is another word for commitment which leads to self-discipline. Without self-discipline there is no action, no change, or at best a half-hearted effort. It is a key difference between successful people and those who merely have lofty aspirations.

Resilience

Resilience is the ability to come back from failure and defeat. If you decide to do hard things, you will fail. In fact, if you haven't experienced failure, you probably haven't challenged yourself enough.

Frederick had no shortage of setbacks. As soon as he learned the basics of reading, his instruction was stopped. The day of his intended escape he and his friends were betrayed and hauled off to jail. After his relatively easy time in Baltimore his new master didn't like his attitude and he was sent to a man known for breaking the spirit of slaves.

What did he do? He didn't give up. He didn't stop believing, he didn't lose heart. Whatever it is we want to achieve, we shouldn't expect it to be easy. Failure is part of the journey. Resilience means that when we come upon setbacks and obstacles, we take them in stride. Life rarely works out exactly as we have planned. When that happens, it's an opportunity to practice resilience and not lose heart.

Resolve, resilience and responsibility were essential elements in Frederick's pursuit of freedom, as they are for anyone pursuing a life of freedom.

Together they make up an inner strength, and freedom requires strength.

Freedom Requires Strength

There are three obstacles that freedom forces us to face. It takes strength to overcome them.

The first obstacle is *the addiction problem*. When we are ruled by harmful habits—and there are many—we need to develop the inner strength to change them. This includes addiction to substances, like alcohol, tobacco and other drugs, but also to habits like fear, anger, negative self-talk and other ways in which our mind and emotions limit our freedom.

The second obstacle is *the authority problem*. We are inclined to accept the opinions and submit to the will of those with authority. When we live in a society that condones slavery or other immoral practices, we need to develop the strength to stand against this. In Fred's case whoever was his master was the authority. Although he physically had no choice but to submit, he didn't accept the authority of the white men who owned him, no matter how many times they told him he was a slave.

The third obstacle is *the slavery problem*. This comes up whenever a person or group imposes their will on another. This obstacle is related to the authority problem, but different because it includes force and coercion. Overcoming this obstacle means we need to defend ourselves against those who try to impose their will on us. Frederick resolved to fight back against Covey. He stood up for himself. It had an incredible effect on him. He recounted that "It rekindled in my breast the smoldering embers of liberty."

There is a constant tension between our desire for freedom and the restrictions placed on us by individuals and groups who have the power to do so. It seems wrong, and in an absolute sense it is wrong. Yet at the same time it helps us build an inner strength that would be hard to come by in any other way.

The desire for freedom was a strong force in Cecil's life too.

Cecil's $100,000 Choice

He wanted to be in theater. His whole family lived and breathed it, so when an opportunity to work as an actor opened up, he took it.

"There is no better training in self-confidence than appearing on a stage, and I needed self-confidence."

This self-confidence served him well when he and three of his friends decided to embark on an adventure. All of them were ready for something new. Cecil and Jesse worked in theater, Sam was a successful glove salesman and Arthur a lawyer.

Together they decided to strike out and make it in the new, up-and-coming motion picture industry. Their first motion picture—they were not yet called movies then—was *The Squaw Man*. It grossed more than twice the cost of filming it, and they were off and running.

Cecil, who directed it, went on to direct seventy movies over the span of his career, creating epics like *The Ten Commandments* with Yul Brynner and *Cleopatra* starring Claudette Colbert.

He was a storyteller. Although he directed plenty of westerns and lighthearted comedies, he loved to tell stories that were meaningful to him, stories connected to his faith.

But the story that most speaks about his dedication to freedom, and to what he considered to be just, was never told on the big screen. It was part of his own story.

In 1944 he received a letter from the American Federation of Radio Artists (AFRA). It was one of the unions he belonged to. Besides being a director, he also had a lucrative job at the Lux Radio Theatre, where he had an audience of twenty to thirty million listeners every Monday evening.

The letter informed him that he was being assessed $1 by the union to oppose a proposition that was to appear on the California ballot during the upcoming elections. The proposition, known as Proposition 12, would make it possible for every Californian to have and hold a job, whether he belonged to a union or not. In other words, the proposition when passed would diminish the power of the unions.

Any member who would not pay the assessment would be suspended from membership in the union, and since AFRA had a closed shop contract with the radio industry, he would therefore no longer be able to work in radio.

Cecil liked working in radio. He had been doing it for nine years and enjoyed it. He didn't want to give up the connection with his audience nor the $100,000 a year of income it provided[10]. And yet, the assessment felt wrong to him.

"When I studied Proposition 12, I decided to vote for it. And here my union was demanding that I pay $1 into a political campaign fund to persuade other citizens to vote against Proposition 12: was demanding, in a word, that I cancel my vote with my dollar. Even if I were opposed to Proposition 12, I asked myself, did my union, did any organization, have the right to impose a compulsory political assessment upon any citizen, under pain of the loss of his right to work?"

The obvious course of action was to pay the $1 and let others worry about the principle of the matter. But that's not how Cecil saw it. For him the principle was real, and it mattered a great deal to him. In his mind paying the $1 was wrong and he didn't want to do it.

Nor did he want to hurt the union, so he decided to look for a compromise. He realized that with the size of his audience, and him being banned from the air if he chose not to pay, it would become a national issue that would in all likelihood hurt the union.

He offered to contribute to the union, as a voluntary gift, a number of dollars equal to the number of members in the Los Angeles area, if they would rescind the assessment and return their dollars to the members who paid them under compulsion. The union refused.

"I saw then that the fundamental issue was not Proposition 12. It was an issue of union power: the power to control the individual member's political freedom through control of his right to work."

After talking it over with his wife, he chose to follow his conscience. He was booted out of the union for refusing to pay the

---

[10] Taking inflation into account, $100K in 1944 would be worth more than $1.5M in 2025.

$1 assessment and conducted his last radio show on January 22, 1945.

It shows how strong Cecil felt about the principle of the matter. The principle was freedom, which was worth more to him than money. The way he saw it coercion was wrong, and he wouldn't be a part of it.

The incident sparked an outpouring of support for him, with many people sending him letters and money. The gist of these letters was much the same: *Do something to keep what has happened to you from happening to the rest of us.*

He did. He used the money to start the DeMille Foundation for Political Freedom which actively promoted and supported the passage of Right to Work laws. These laws give men and women the right to work regardless of their membership or lack of membership in a union.

Both Frederick Douglass and Cecil B. DeMille took a stand for freedom. The fight for freedom takes different forms at different times, but for both of them it was deeply personal. And both of them recognized that a system of coercion and compulsion fails the integrity test.

Recognizing the freedom of each individual to make their own choices is an essential component of integrity, but many people don't see it that way. The result is that liberty is always under attack by people who don't believe in freedom. They, of course, want to have it for themselves but believe that for others control and coercion is better. They believe they have a superior vision, and they mean to implement that vision. To them the end justifies the means.

What is Freedom?

All freedom starts with free will. We have freedom to choose what to do with our life. To work hard or to be lazy. To reach for the stars or to go for easy. How to respond when someone treats us unjustly. To be a force for good or not. These choices can't be taken from us.

There is a never-ending tension between our desire for freedom and the reality of the world around us. Not all choices are open to all people. This world does not make it easy for us to become all that we can be. It requires that we build the strength and abilities to overcome resistance—both our own and the limitations imposed on us from the outside—in the same way that a bodybuilder builds his muscles.

Agency is the sum total of the skills, knowledge, and attitudes we have acquired that expand our choices. This includes developing right discrimination—the ability to make good decisions.

Besides agency, which is largely under our own control, there is liberty, which depends on the country and culture we live in. How much freedom we have may depend on things like our gender, our age, our family, and the legal and cultural norms we are subject to. The Human Freedom index[11] defines it as "the absence of coercive constraint." There is no such thing as absolute freedom, the reality is that there are always constraints, but some countries allow for more freedom than others as do some roles and professions.

The final component that affects our freedom is power, and by this I mean how big the potential impact of our actions can be. How much power we have is frequently not fully under our control, but we can increase it by taking on certain roles, and by acquiring skills and money. Both money and other forms of power can increase the options we have, as well as the impact our choices have. Great power also means great responsibility, the flip side of power.

---

[11] An index created by the Fraser Institute and the Cato Institute, that measures the level of freedom worldwide for each country.

30,000 Brushstrokes

Nadav Ben Yehuda came upon his friend a few hundred meters from the top of Mount Everest. That was a defining moment.

You may have had a moment like that too. Perhaps you had to face a fear. Did you confront it, or did you hide? Or maybe it was like Tom when he faced the force of his father-in-law's opinion. What do you say in such a moment? Or Chiune Sugihara who had a direct order from his superiors not to issue visas, and a line with over a thousand Jews outside his door. A defining moment.

In a moment like this, what you choose to do will likely have a deep and lasting impact on your life and the lives of others. A moment of truth. A moment where you define who you are.

Not all moments carry that much meaning, but every day has the potential for us to find meaning and to define who we are.

Most of us will have about 30,000 days, give or take a few thousand. Each day is a brushstroke on the canvas of life. Some brushstrokes will be more meaningful than others. As with any painting, what's more important than each individual brushstroke is the overall painting that emerges.

The question is, what is your painting about? How do you make it meaningful?

Life has a way of bringing that to our attention.

The closer we come to the end of our 30,000 brushstrokes, the bigger the question looms.

Because freedom is the option to choose how to spend our time.

Freedom isn't all that interesting until we decide what to do with it. Then we're creating a story. That's what freedom is, you and I and everyone else, creating our own stories. We write our story with the choices we make. Our choices are simply a reflection of what's meaningful to us.

Whatever we choose to do with our life, we're creating the story of our potential. Freedom is choice, and it matters what we choose. What is the most meaningful thing we can do with our time?

Knowing what is meaningful to you is the most important thing in the world. If you don't know what it is, it's worth it to put some effort into finding out.

Meaningful success means finding out what really matters to you and then putting in the necessary effort to make it happen. This is how you define who you are.

That's the heart of freedom.

Summary

- Freedom comes with responsibility and has to be earned.

- Freedom's four components:
  - **Free will** – The ability to choose what to do, how to act and how not to act.
  - **Liberty** – The absence of coercive constraints, like written and unwritten rules imposed on us by society and the groups we are members of.
  - **Agency** – The combination of commitment, skills, knowledge and beliefs that can expand our options, and therefore our freedom.
  - **Power** – The ability to effect change on the people and things in our environment and in ourselves. The more power, the larger the effect we can have, and therefore the greater the responsibility.

- Three obstacles we need to overcome to gain freedom:
  - Authority problem – Uncritical acceptance of opinions and submission to the will of those with

authority.

- Slavery problem – One person or group of people imposing their will on another person or group.
- Addiction problem – Limiting our choices due to the inability to break free from harmful habits.

- Freedom requires strength
  - to overcome addiction to negative habits (addiction problem)
  - to go against authority when needed (authority problem)
  - to resist or protect against outside forces trying to bend us to their will (slavery problem)

- Freedom is an essential element of integrity. When we deny someone the freedom they deserve, we are acting without integrity.

- The heart of freedom is our ability to define who we are. We do this through the choices we make.

Afterword

This is a book about ideas and principles, but it's also about the real world. I explore ideas and reframe existing beliefs. Do they lead to success? The proof of the pudding is in the eating. These ideas can be tested, and I encourage you to do so.

Are they useful and are they true? If they are, you have a principle to guide you.

Ideas are like cars. You can go to the dealer and fall in love right there with the shiny machine on the showroom floor, but before you buy it, don't you want to take it out for a spin?

See how it handles on the road, how it takes curves (life does throw us curveballs after all) and how it handles on the highway. Do the brakes work? A car may be a status symbol for some, but for most of us the car is practical. It helps you take the kids to school, do groceries and go to soccer practice. It needs to work and do its job. If it does the job well it gives you more freedom.

The same is true for the ideas in this book. They have to work, and if they do their job well, they give you more freedom.

Life is for living, and ideally, for living to the fullest. Test out the ideas in this book. See if they work. These ideas aren't revolutionary; they're evolutionary. We have the ability to evolve and grow.

This evolution has a general direction, but the way it happens, the way we move in that direction, is a little bit different for each of us. We each grow in our own way and in our own time.

I hope you'll try out these ideas. I hope you'll test them. If I'm right, you'll find some guidelines on how to be a force for good.

There isn't one way to be a force for good, there are many. In fact, there are as many ways as there are people. There are also an equal number of ways to go in the other direction.

It's a choice, and my hope is that this book makes the choice a little bit clearer and easier.

I love to hear from my readers! If you have a story to share or want to let me know how this book has impacted you, drop me a line through my website at francisdegeus.com.

If you enjoyed reading this book, consider leaving a review on Amazon.com.
It would make my day!

Acknowledgments

While writing a book is a big undertaking, it is only the beginning. It takes countless hours of revising, editing and incorporating feedback from early readers to make the book the best it can be.

All stories in the book are from real people, although some names were changed to protect people's privacy.

I want to express my gratitude to a number of people.

To Daniel Chappell, Gina Curley, Walter Williams, Jeannette Mueller, and Todd Temkin, my deepest gratitude for taking the time to answer my questions and trusting me with your stories.

I also want to thank Kimberly Young, Roy Ludwick, Hugh Curley, Dave Walden, Joycelyn Calvin-White, and Raphaelle Calvin for reading an early version of this book and providing me with valuable feedback.

Special thanks goes to Helaine Reiner, my wife and partner in life, for reading early chapters of the book, giving me feedback, and her continuing patience with me while I was working on the book.

To Willie, my twenty-pound dog, who quite literally supported me while writing the book by worming himself between my lower back and the back of my chair.

And to the spiritual teachers who were my source of inspiration, insight and support, often in the middle of the night, helping me to better understand what I was writing about.

Notes

Introduction

Report on Spirituality Among Americans, Pew Research Center. https://www.pewresearch.org/religion/2023/12/07/spirituality-among-americans/

Man's Search for Meaning (Boston: Beacon Press, 2006) by Victor Frankl.

1. What is Meaningful Success?

The Snowball (New York: Bantam Books, 2008) by Alice Schroeder.

Walter Williams' story is based on a personal interview with the author.

Mountain States Children's Home website: https://www.msch.org/

A validation study on the Multidimensional Adolescent Assessment Scale can be accessed on ResearchGate, https://www.researchgate.net/publication/249681300_The_Multidimensional_Adolescent_Assessment_Scale_A_Validation_Study/link/56ab54da08ae8f386569583o/download?_tp=eyJjb250ZXh0Ijp7ImZpcnN0UGFnZSI6InB1YmxpY2F0aW9uIiwicGFnZSI6InB1YmxpY2F0aW9uIn19.

The Inner Scorecard and accompanying questionnaire were created by the author.

2. The Head, the Heart and You

My Stroke of Insight (New York, Penguin Group, 2006) by Jill Bolte Taylor.

Figure 2.1 was created by the author.

The Heart Speaks (New York, Touchstone, 2006) by Dr. Mimi Guarneri.

The use of HU as a spiritual technique is an ancient tradition that has been used throughout history. More information about this ancient mantra can be found at https://www.eckankar.org/experience/hu-the-sound-of-soul/

The Map Gallery for New York City can be found at https://www.nyc.gov/nyc resources/nyc-maps.page.

3. The Key to Mastery and Excellence

Black and White (New York, Simon and Schuster, 2014) by Richard Williams.

Figure 3.1 was created by the author.

On The Line, (New York, Grand Central Publishing, 2009) by Serena Williams.

A short video clip of the ABC News interview with fourteen-year-old Venus Williams can be found on YouTube: https://www.youtube.com/watch?v=IZ_Dgnn437o.

4. The Power of Principles

Isaac Newton (New York, Pantheon Books, 2003) by James Gleick.

A Short History of Nearly Everything (New York, Broadway Books, 2003) by Bill Bryson.

On The Line (New York, Grand Central Publishing, 2009) by Serena Williams.

5. The Maturity Principle

The Lucifer Effect (New York, Random House, 2008) by Philip G. Zimbardo.

The Child and Reality (New York, Grossman Publishers, 1973) by Jean Piaget.

Figure 5.1 was created by the author.

Lance Armstrong interview with Oprah Winfrey aired in January 2013 on OWN.

Interview with David Walsh on Global Cycling Network https://www.youtube.com/watch?v=bkARvYIwT8E

Figure 5.2 was created by the author.

The 5/23/2012 article in the Times of Israel:
https://www.timesofisrael.com/he-was-waiting-for-the-end-israeli-climber-describes-how-he-saved-turkish-friend-on-everest/

6. Closing the Authority Gap

Jeannette's story is based on a personal interview with the author.

Milgram's experiment.
https://www.simplypsychology.org/milgram.html
https://en.wikipedia.org/wiki/Milgram_experiment

DVD, *Sugihara – Conspiracy of Kindness* (WGBH Boston Video, 2005)

A special fate: Chiune Sugihara, hero of the Holocaust (New York, Scholastic Press, 2000) by Alison Leslie Gold.

The Just: How six unlikely heroes saved thousands of Jews from the Holocaust (Minneapolis, Scribe Publications, 2021) by Jan Brokken.

7. The Moral Compass

Parable about the Secret of Power was created by the author.

Personal History (New York, Vintage Books, 1998, 1997) by Katharine Graham.

History.com article on the Nixon White House tapes.
https://www.history.com/articles/nixon-secret-tapes-quotes-

scandal-watergate

8. Life, Our Personal Obstacle Course

Daniel's story is based on a personal interview with the author.

The Autobiography of Benjamin Franklin (Garden City, Dover Publications, 1996) by Benjamin Franklin.

Gina's story is based on a personal interview with the author.

George Dantzig: https://malevus.com/george-dantzig/

9. The Integrity Model: A Blueprint for Success

The Price of Loyalty (New York, Simon and Schuster, 2004) by Ron Suskind.

Paul O'Neill Speech to Healthcare CEOs on "The Irreducible Components of Leadership": https://www.youtube.com/watch?v=htLCVqaLBvo

Paul O'Neill on Safety Leadership: https://www.youtube.com/watch?v=0gvOrYuPBEA

Paul O'Neill CEO of Alcoa - It's all about safety: https://www.youtube.com/watch?v=tC2ucDs_XJY

Lasting Impact: Leaders Share Lessons From Paul H. O'Neill, Sr. (Pittsburgh, Value Capture, LLC., 2020) by George Taninecz.

A Playbook for Habitual Excellence: A Leader's Roadmap From the Life and Work of Paul H. O'Neill, Sr. (Value Capture, LLC., 2022)

Seek True North: Stories on Leadership and Ethics - Bill O'Rourke on YouTube
https://www.youtube.com/watch?v=bmFDXecIqJM

Streams in the Desert: 366 daily Devotional Readings (Grand Rapids, Zondervan, 1997) by L.B. Cowman.

Last Call: The Rise and Fall of Prohibition (New York, Scribner, 2010) by Daniel Okrent.

The War on Alcohol: Prohibition and the Rise of the American State (New York, W.W. Norton & Company, 2016) by Lisa McGirr.

Figure 9.1 was created by the author.

Figure 9.2 was created by the author.

Figure 9.3 was created by the author.

Figure 9.4 was created by the author.

10. Love, the Heart of Success

Tom's story is based on a personal interview with the author.

https://www.c-span.org/clip/public-affairs-event/justice-ginsburg-on-her-friendship-with-justice-scalia/4541673

https://www.aspeninstitute.org/events/justiceruthbaderginsburg/

https://www.fox26houston.com/news/ruth-bader-ginsburg-and-antonin-scalia-an-unlikely-friendship-and-an-elephant-ride-in-india

Todd's story is based on a personal interview with the author.

11. Sorting Facts From Fiction

Modern flat Earth beliefs on Wikipedia:
https://en.wikipedia.org/wiki/Modern_flat_Earth_beliefs

Interview with Dan Shechtman:
https://www.theguardian.com/science/2013/jan/06/dan-shechtman-nobel-prize-chemistry-interview

GrassrootsHealth: https://www.grassrootshealth.net/

Berkshire Hathaway vs SP 500 - Business Insider:
https://www.businessinsider.com/warren-buffett-berkshire-hathaway-vs-sp-500-2015-3

Figure 11.1 Ninio's Extinction Illusion. Named after its creator, Jacques Ninio.

Figure 11.2 Ninio's Extinction Illusion with gridlines removed by the author.

Figure 11.3 was created by the author.

Factfulness (New York, Flatiron Books, 2018) by Hans Rosling.

Ignaz Semmelweiss:
https://www.britannica.com/biography/Ignaz-Semmelweis

12. 30,000 Brushstrokes

The Life and Times of Frederick Douglass (New York, Cosimo Classics, 2008) by Frederick Douglass.

The Autobiography of Cecil B. DeMille (Prentice-Hall, 1959) by Cecil B. DeMille.

The Human Freedom Index 2024:
https://www.cato.org/sites/cato.org/files/2024-12/2024-human-freedom-index.pdf

www.ingramcontent.com/pod-product-compliance
Lightning Source LLC
LaVergne TN
LVHW051050080426
835508LV00019B/1804